OTT FORESMAN • ADDISON WESLEY

Mathematics

Kindergarten

Practice Masters/Workbook

Editorial Offices: Glenview, Illinois • Parsippany, New Jersey • New York, New York

Sales Offices: Parsippany, New Jersey • Duluth, Georgia • Glenview, Illinois
Coppell, Texas • Ontario, California • Mesa, Arizona

Overview

Practice Masters/Workbook provides additional practice on the concept or concepts taught in each lesson.

ISBN 0-328-04952-2

2 3 4 5 6 7 8 9 10 V084 09 08 07 06 05 04 03

Name ______________________________

Inside and Outside

P 1-1

Directions Have children circle the bear and the rabbit outside the wagon. Have them circle the dog and the fish inside the wagon.

Name ______________________________

Over, Under, and On

P 1-2

Directions Have children mark an *X* on the cat and the bird on the chair, the mouse under the chair, and the spider over the chair.

Name ______________________________

Top, Middle, and Bottom

P 1-3

Directions Have children mark an *X* on the apple on the bottom, the orange on the top, and the banana in the middle.

Name ______________________________

Left and Right

P 1-4

Left	Right

Directions Have children color the bird on the right blue, the puppy on the left brown, the fish on the right orange, and the kitten on the left yellow.

Name ____________________

Same and Different

P 1-5

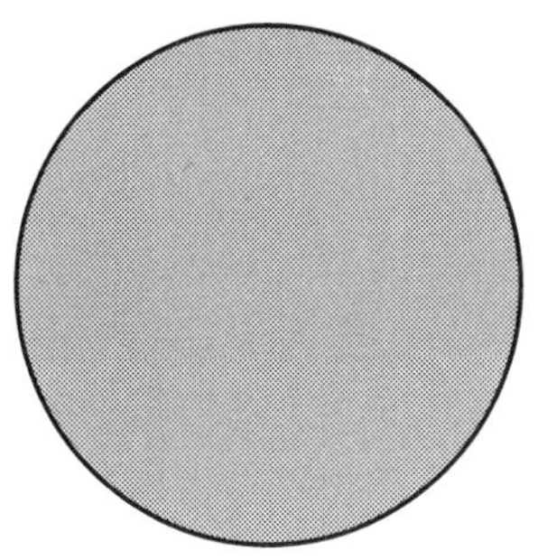
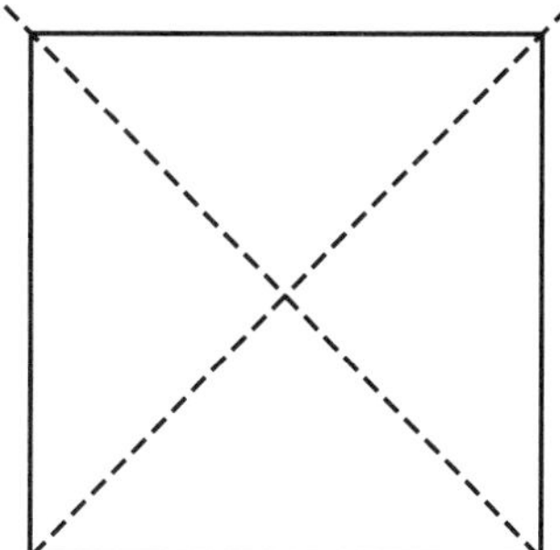
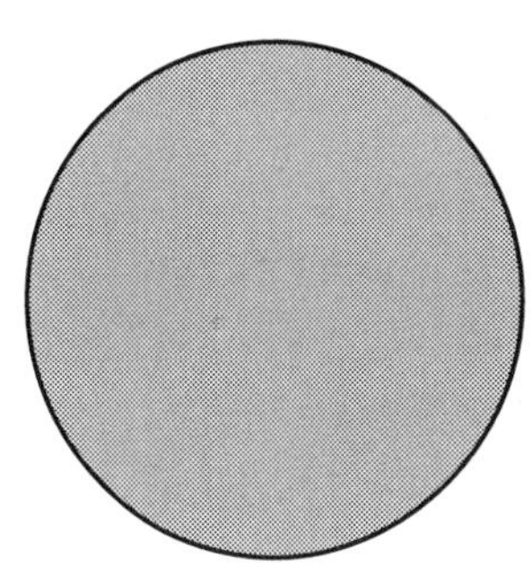

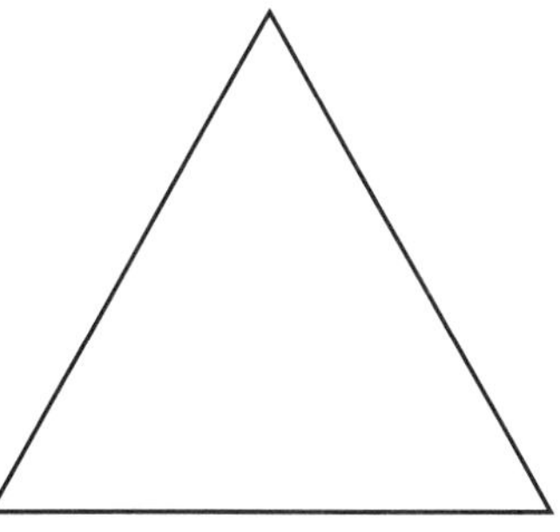

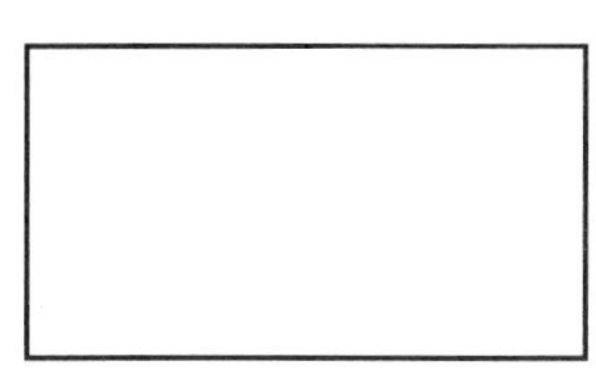

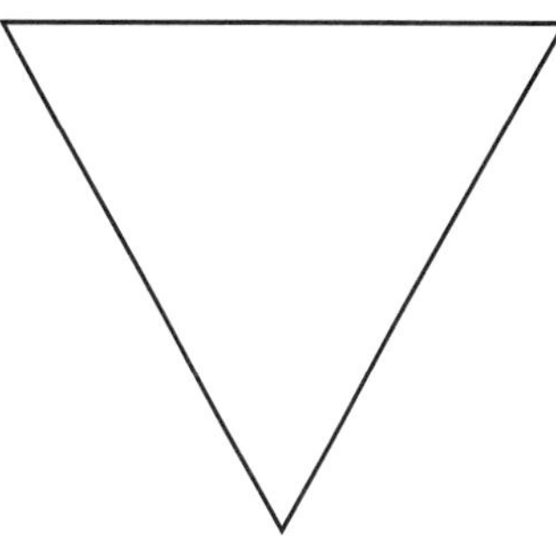

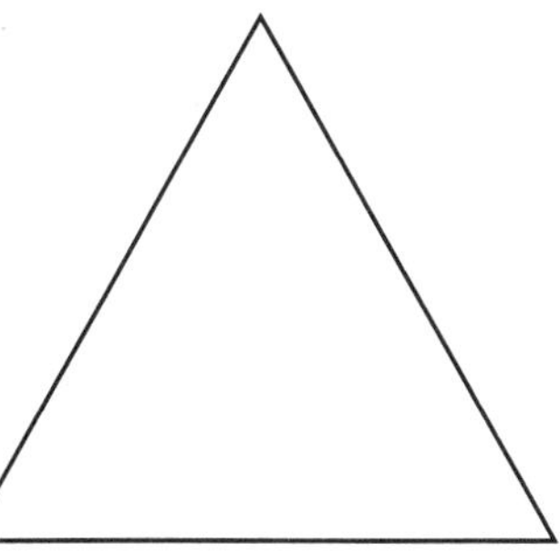
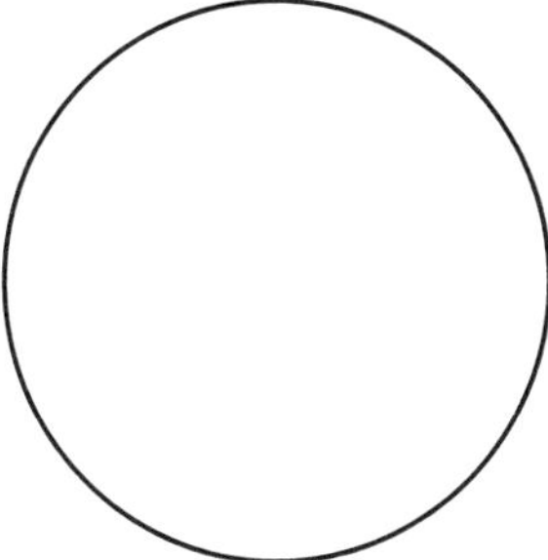
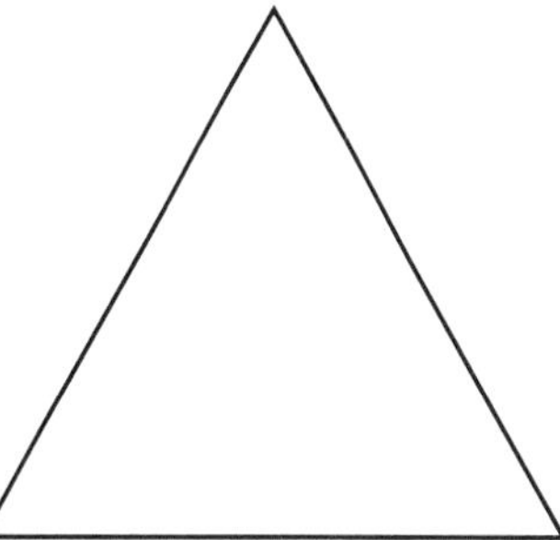

Directions Have children color the same two items in each row the same color. Have them mark an *X* on the item in each row that is different from the other two items.

Name ______________________________

Sorting by One Attribute

P 1-6

Directions Have children sort the cats and the fish by drawing lines to the appropriate circles.

Name ______________________________

Sorting the Same Set in Different Ways

1

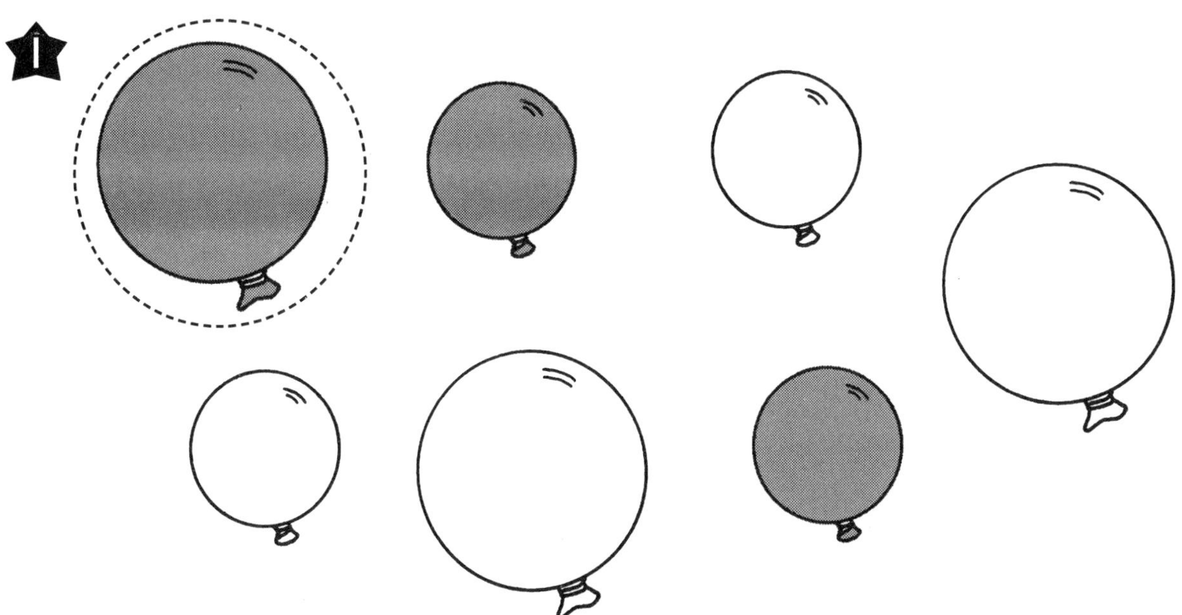

2

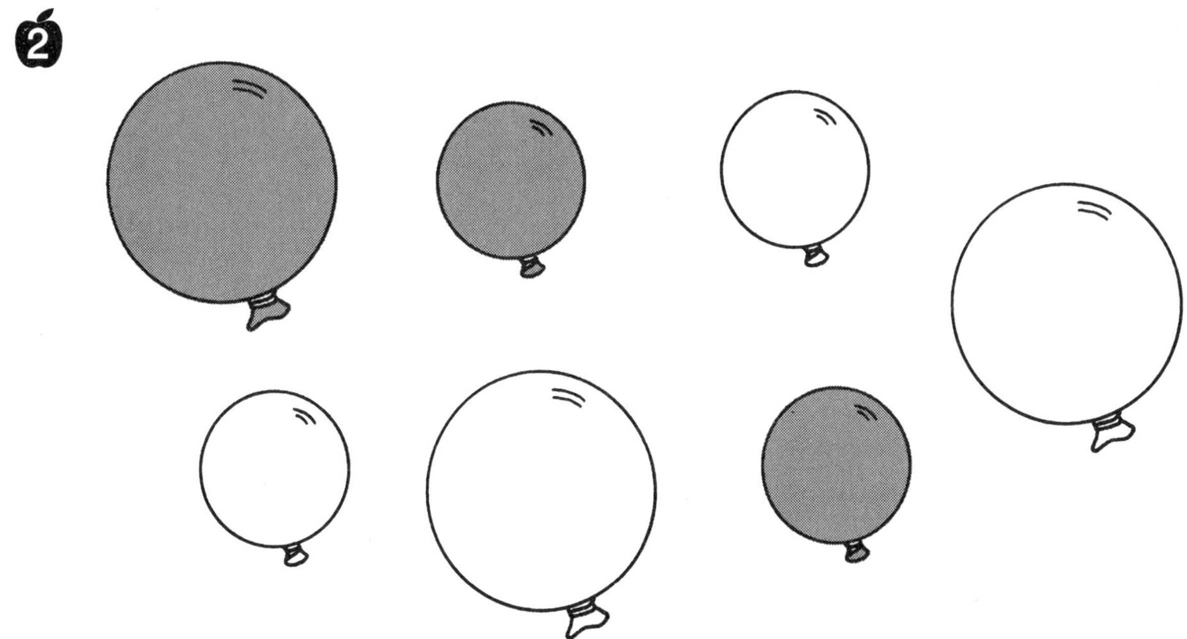

Directions Have children sort the balloons by circling all the large balloons in Exercise 1 and by circling all the shaded balloons in Exercise 2.

Name ____________________

Sorting by More Than One Attribute

P 1-8

1

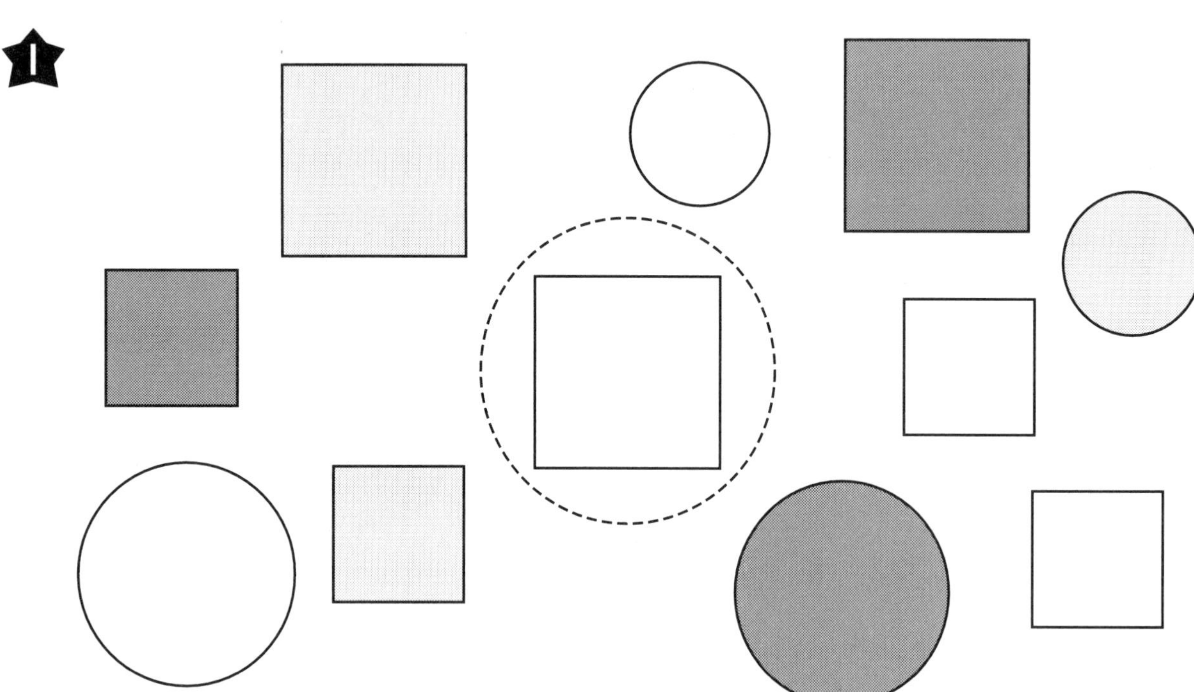

2

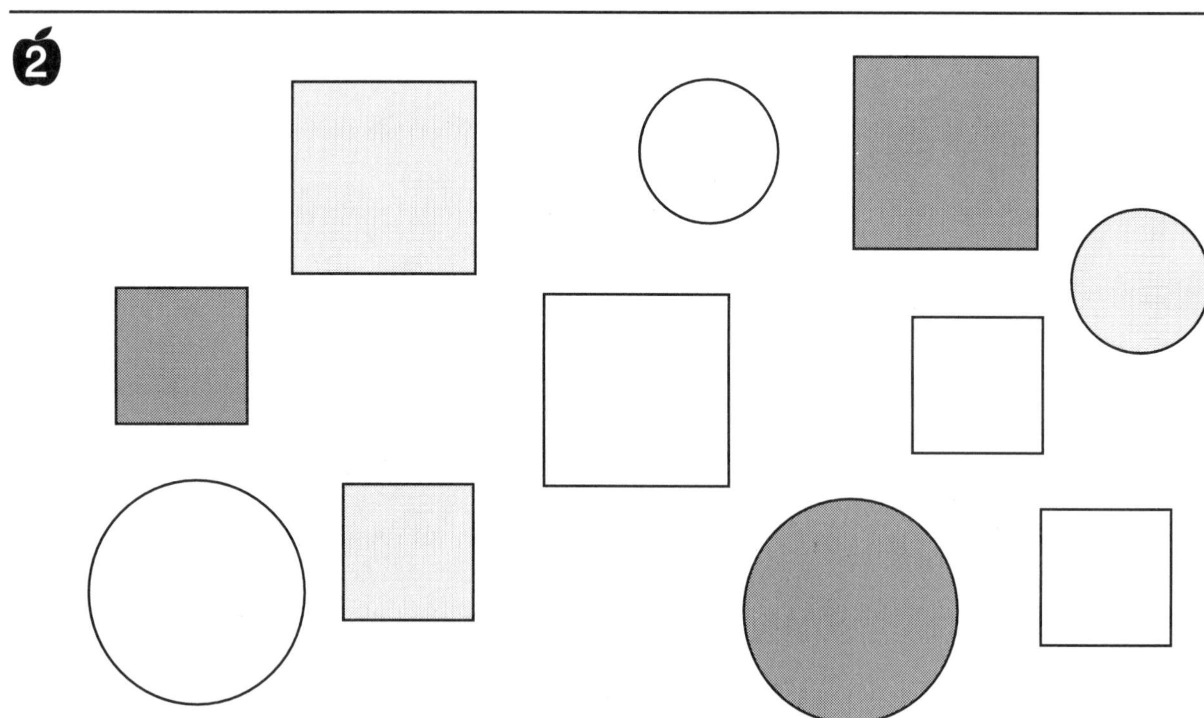

Directions Have children sort the shapes by circling all the white squares in Exercise 1 and all the small circles in Exercise 2.

Name ______________________________

PROBLEM-SOLVING STRATEGY **P 1-9**

Use Logical Reasoning

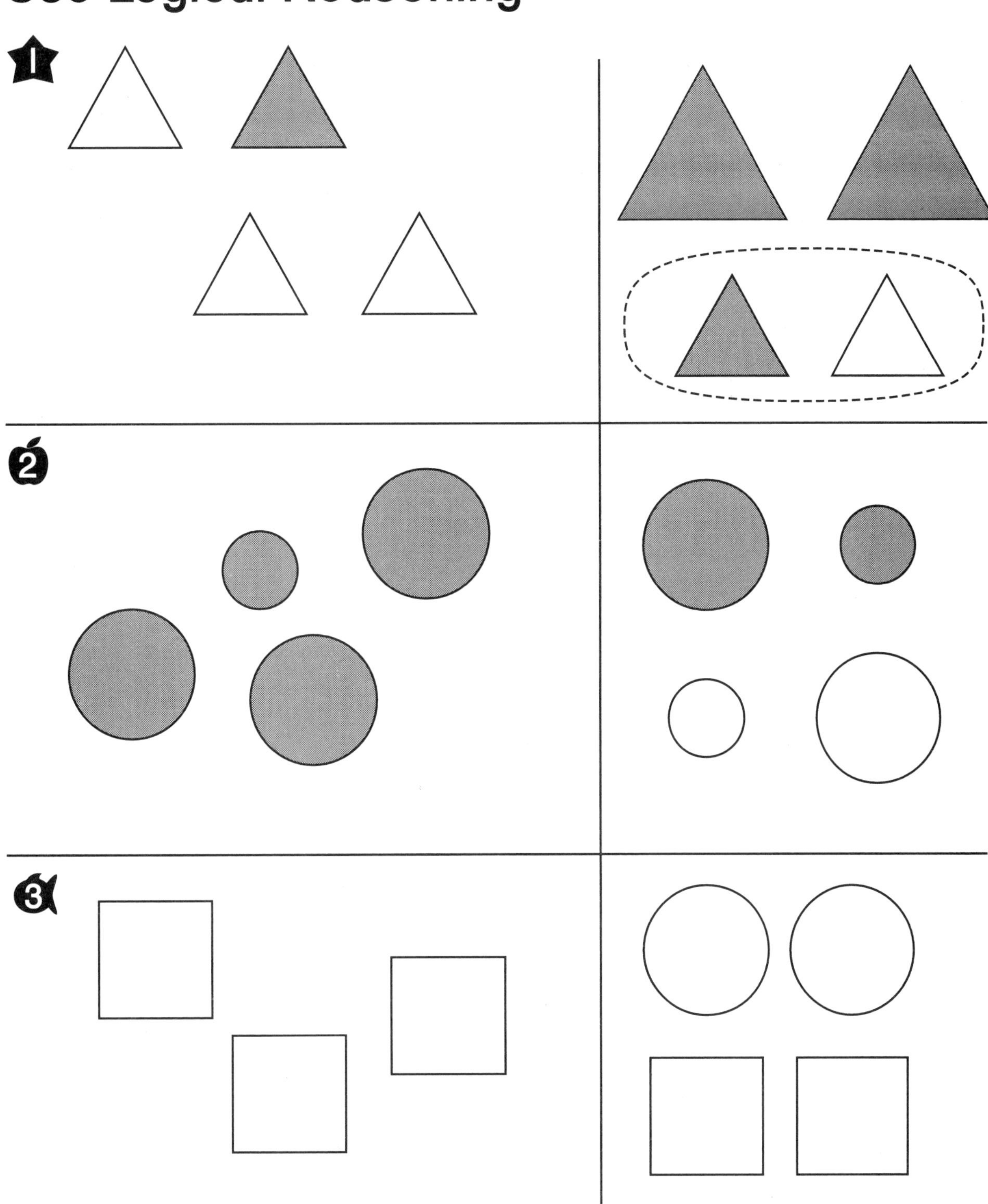

Directions For each exercise have children identify how the attribute blocks are sorted and circle the blocks that show the sorting rule.

Name ______________________________

PROBLEM-SOLVING APPLICATIONS **P 1-10**

Take a Close Look

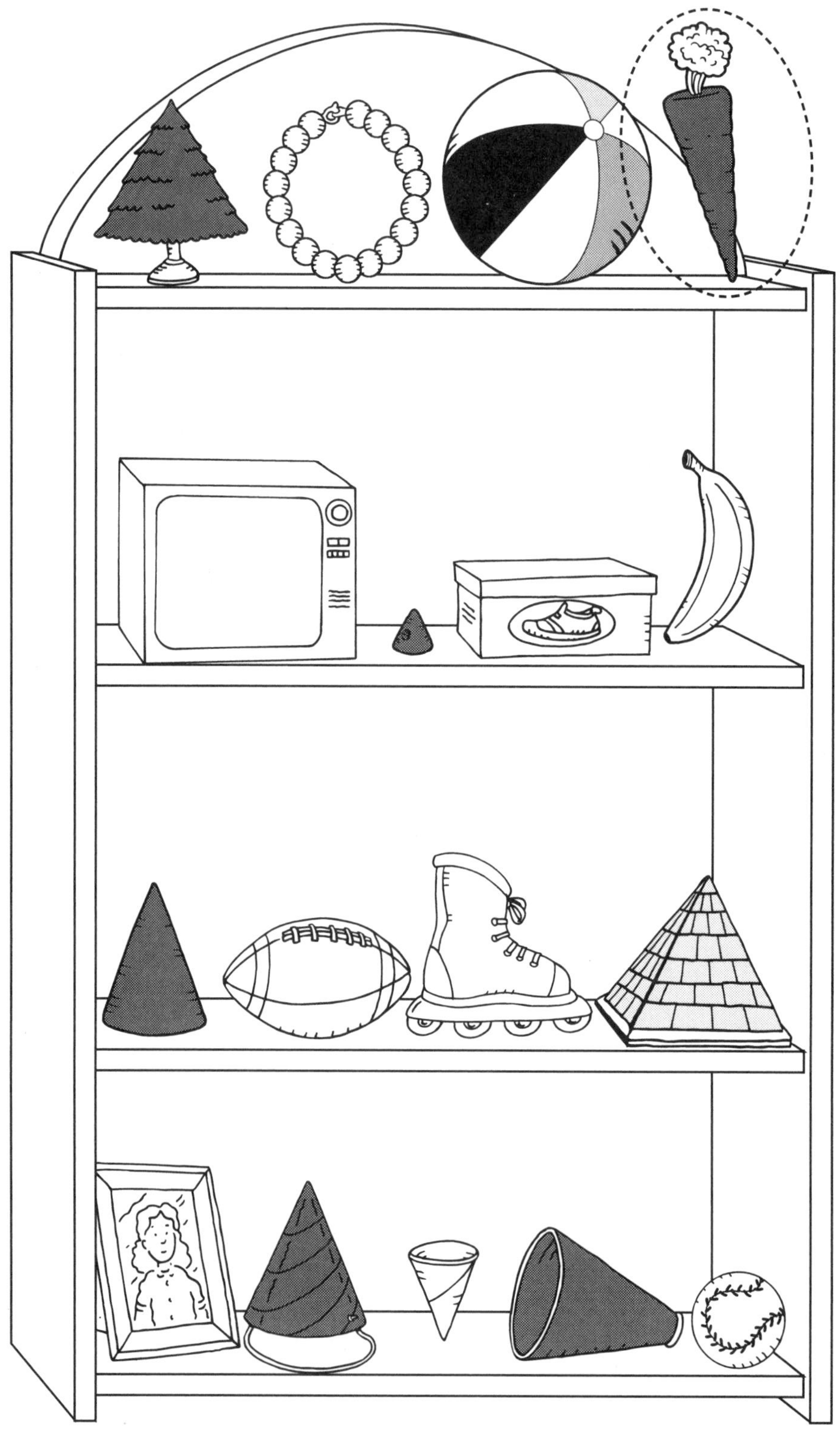

Directions Have children circle the object over the banana, circle the object under the football, circle the object to the left of the necklace, put an *X* on the object to the right of the skate, and put an *X* on the object under the beach ball.

Name ______________________

As Many, More, and Fewer

P 2-1

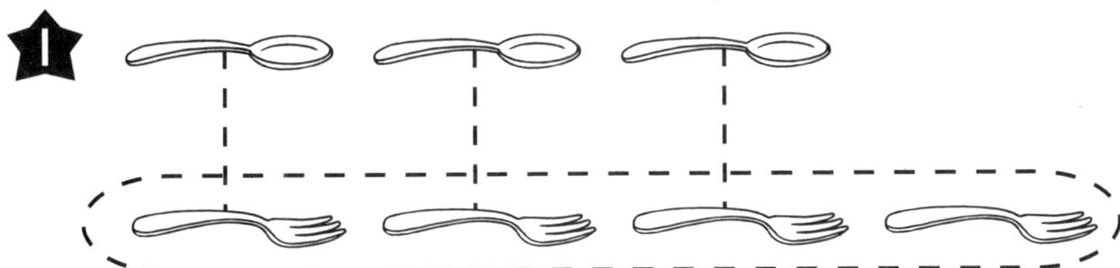

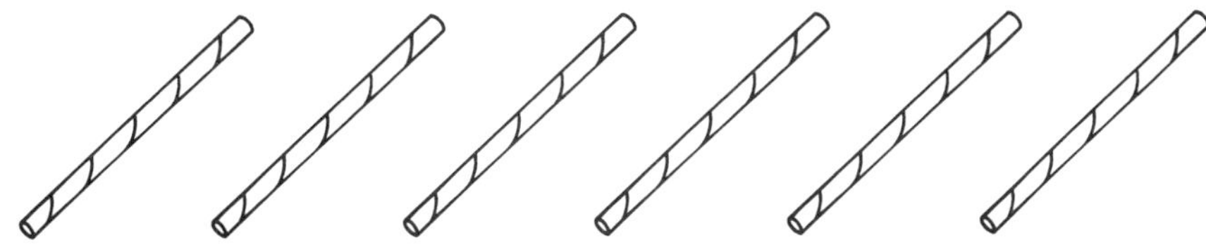

Directions In each exercise have children draw a line from each item in the top row to each item in the bottom row and circle the row with more.

Name ___________________________________

Real Graphs

P 2-2

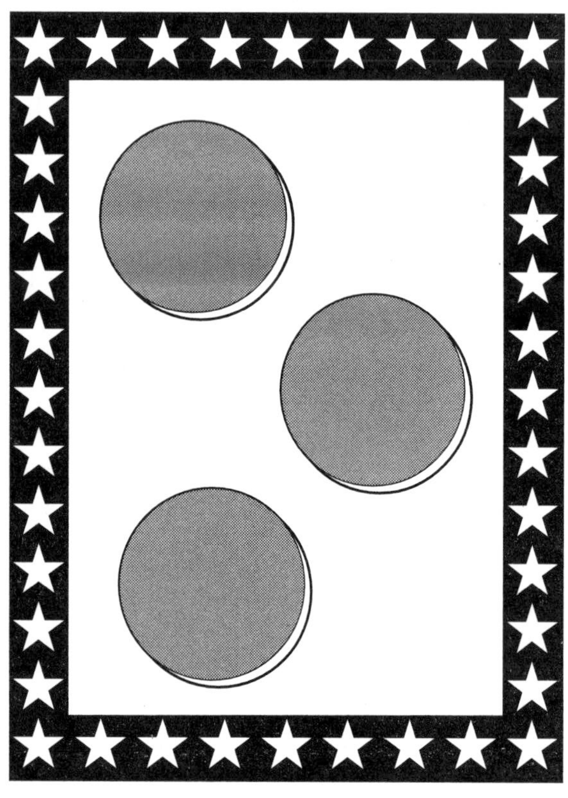

Which has Fewer?

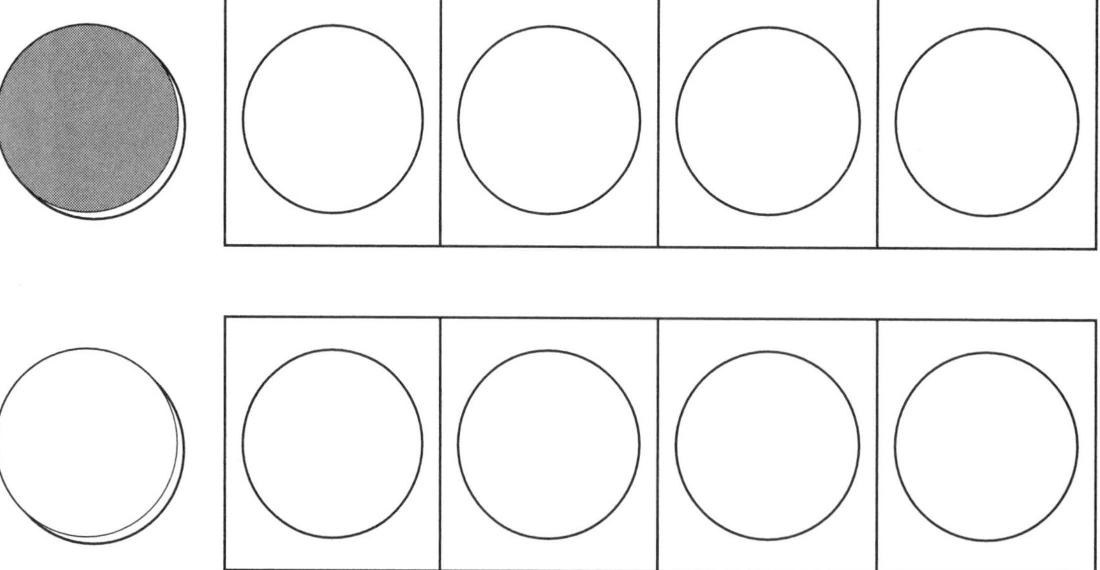

Directions Have children place matching counters on the workmat. Then have them move the counters to the graphs and color the rows to show the counters. Have them circle the row that has fewer counters.

Name ____________________

Picture Graphs

Toys on the Shelves

Directions Have children look at the pigs, ducks, and rabbits on the shelves. Have them color a picture on the graph for each toy.

Name ____________________

Bar Graphs

P 2-4

Which Drink Do We Like Better?

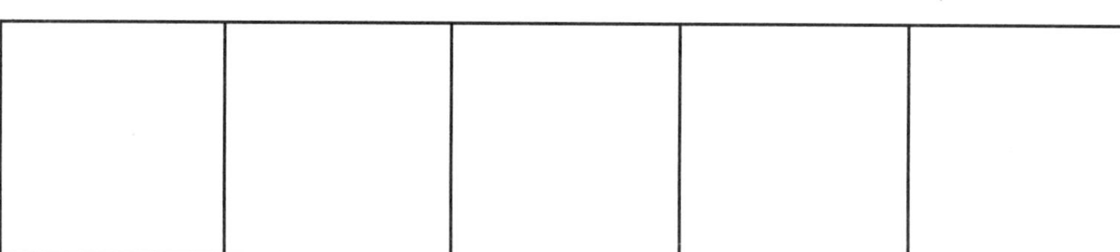

Directions Have children survey some classmates to decide which drink they like better: milk or juice. Have them color a square on the graph for each response. Then have children answer the survey question by circling the drink that more children like better.

Name ______________________________

Sound and Movement Patterns

P 2-5

2

3

4

Directions Have children circle the instrument that comes next in the pattern.

Name ______________________________

Color Patterns

P 2-6

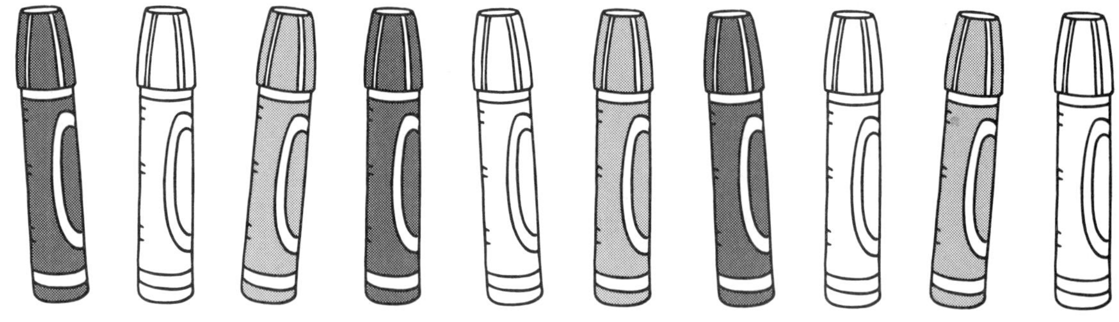

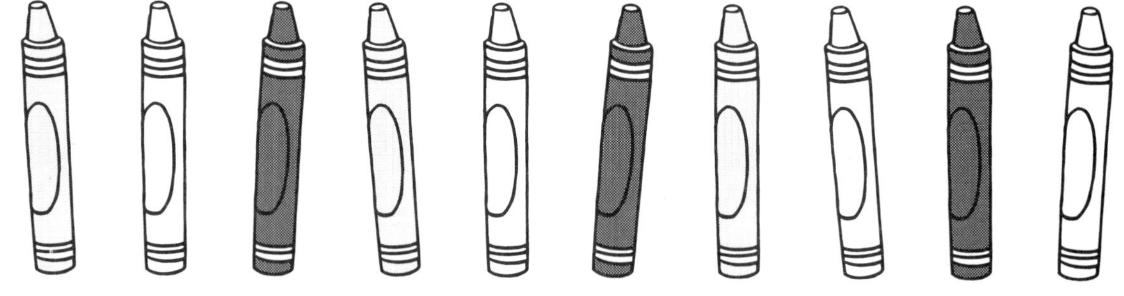

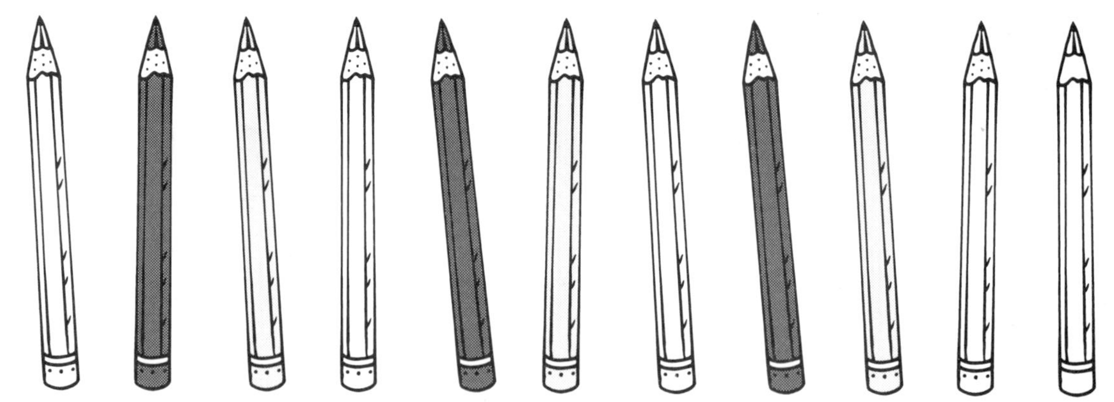

Directions Have children color the objects at the end of each row to show which colors come next in the patterns.

Name ______________________________

Shape Patterns

P 2-7

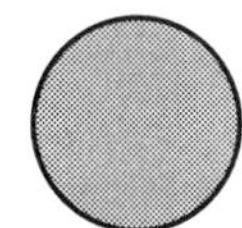 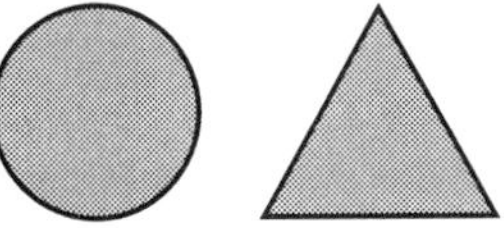 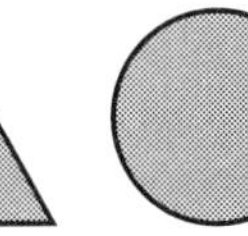 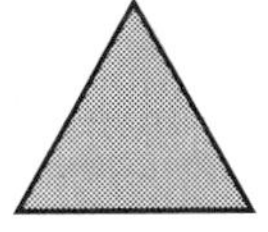 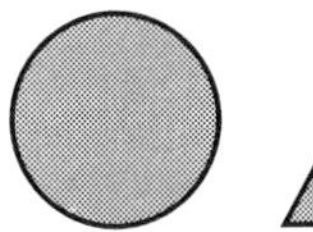 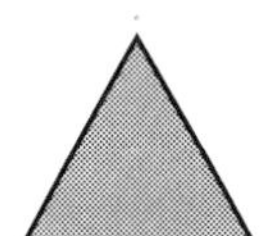

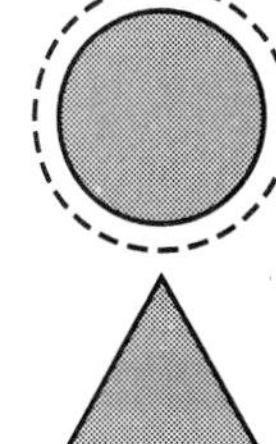

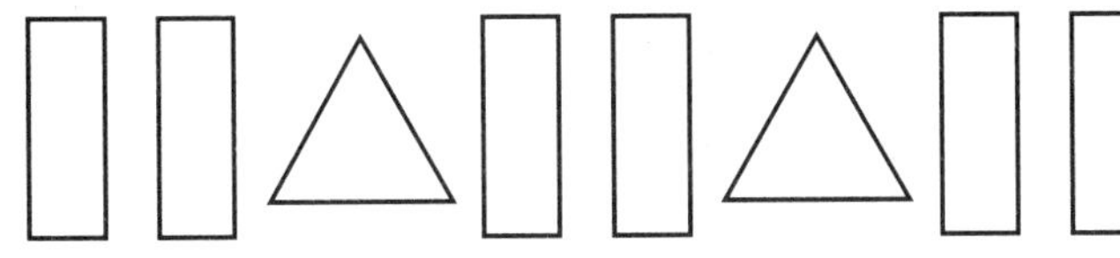 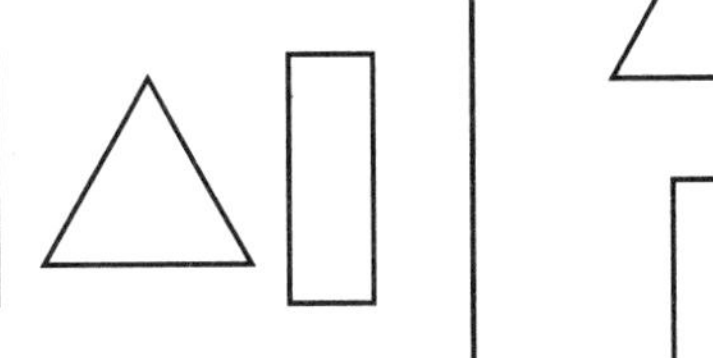

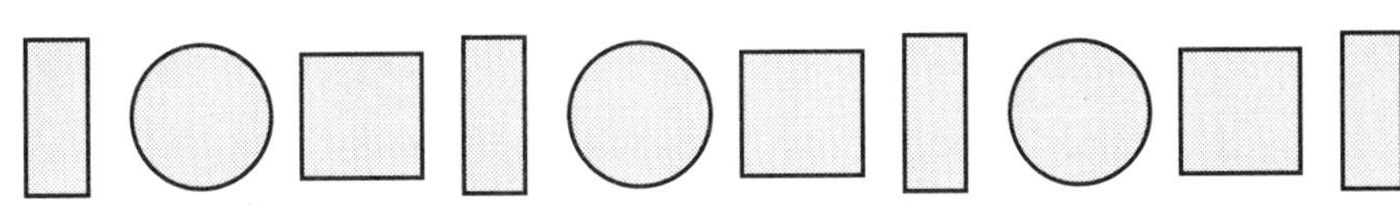 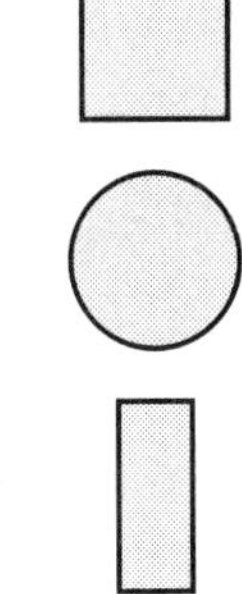

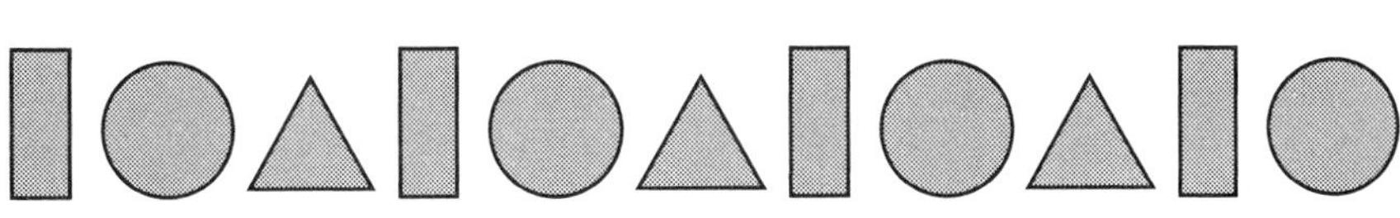 

Directions Have children circle the shape that comes next in the pattern.

Name ______________________________

Comparing Patterns

P 2-8

1

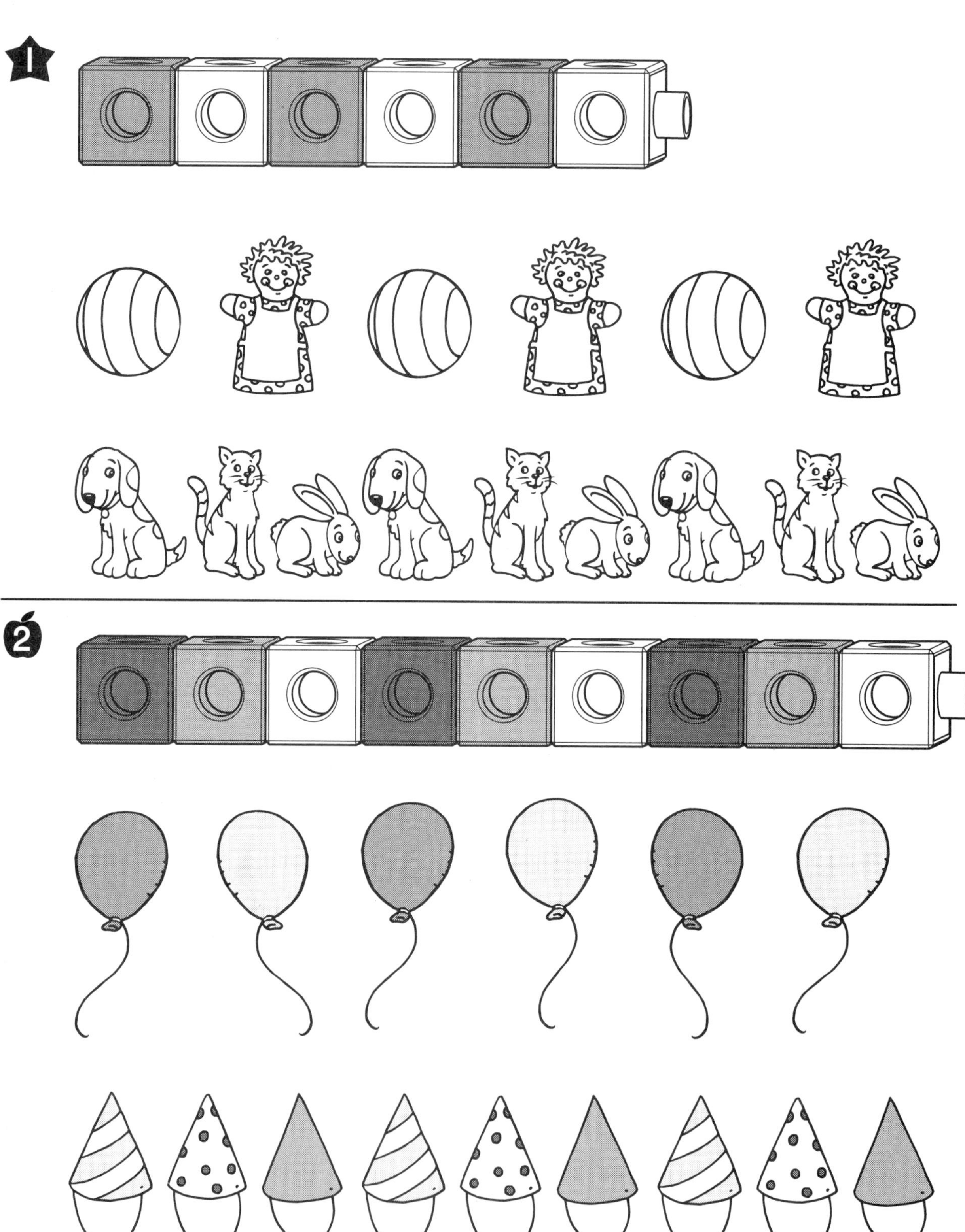

2

Directions Have children circle the pattern that matches the cube pattern at the top of each exercise.

Name ______

PROBLEM-SOLVING STRATEGY **P 2-9**

Look for a Pattern

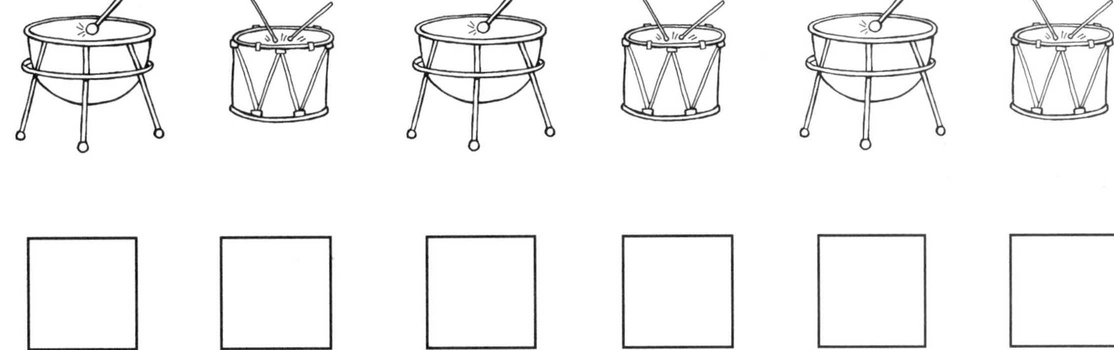

Directions For each exercise have children circle where the pattern repeats. Then have children show the pattern in another way by coloring the squares.

Name ___________________________

Creating Patterns

P 2-10

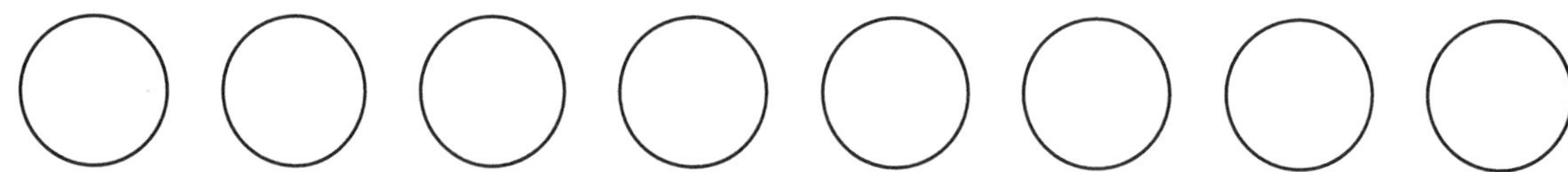

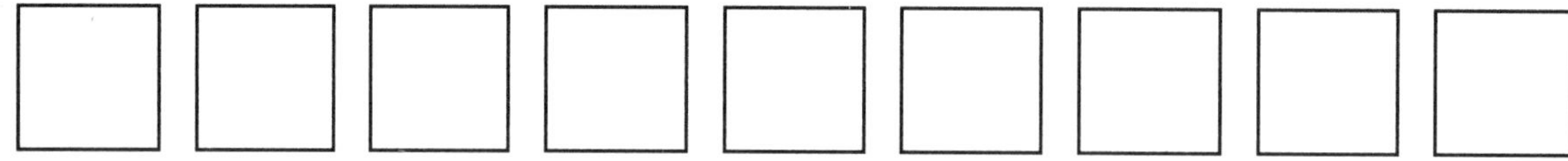

Directions Exercise 1: Have children use two-color counters to make patterns and then color circles to match their patterns. Exercise 2: Have children use color tiles to make patterns and then color squares to match their patterns. Exercise 3: Have children make patterns with counters and tiles and then draw and color the patterns.

Name ______________________________

Favorite Things

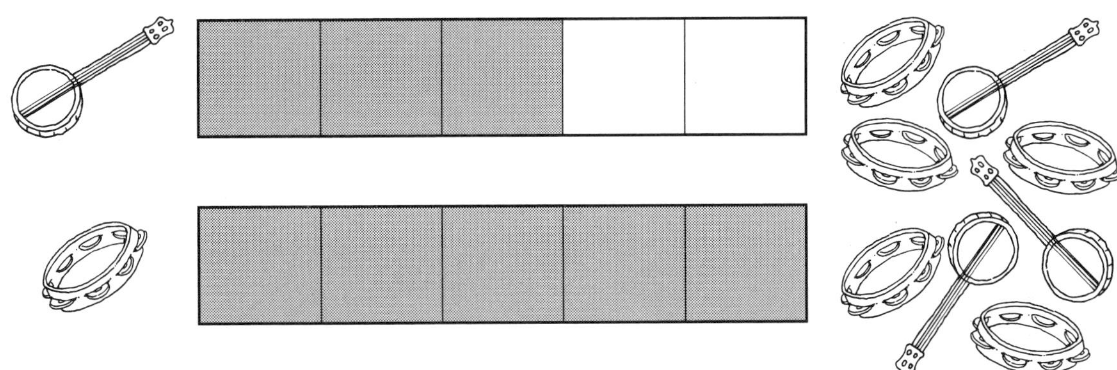

Directions Exercise 1: Tell children that Heidi made a graph to show instruments her friends like. Which instrument do more children like? Have children circle that instrument. Exercises 2 and 3: Tell children that Luis likes to make patterns with his toys. Ask children to look at each pattern and decide what pattern Luis made. Have children circle the repeating part of each pattern.

Name ____________________

Counting 1, 2, and 3

P 3-1

Directions Have pairs of children count each bird group and color a square for each bird in a group. Then have partners tell number stories about the bird groups.

Name ______________________________

Reading and Writing 1, 2, and 3

P 3-2

1

2

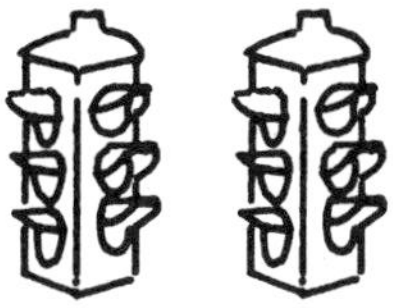

3

4

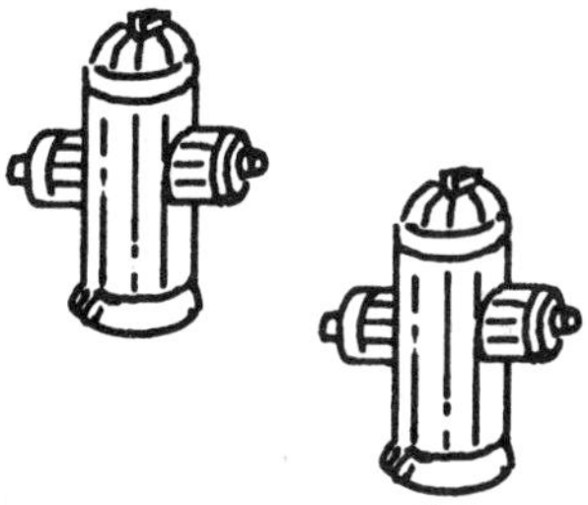

5

Directions Have children count each group and practice writing the number.

Name ______________________________

Counting 4 and 5

P 3-3

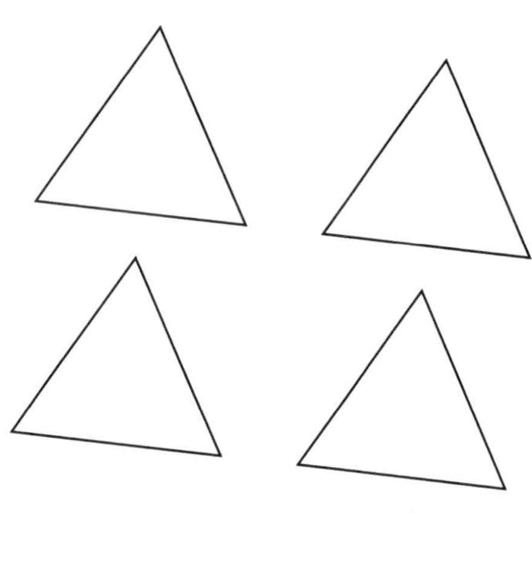

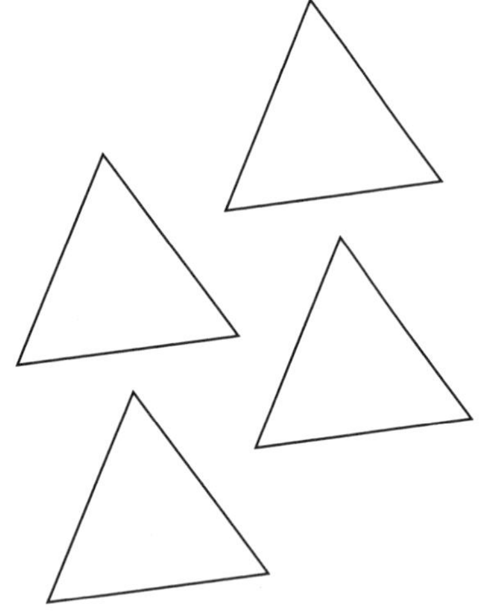

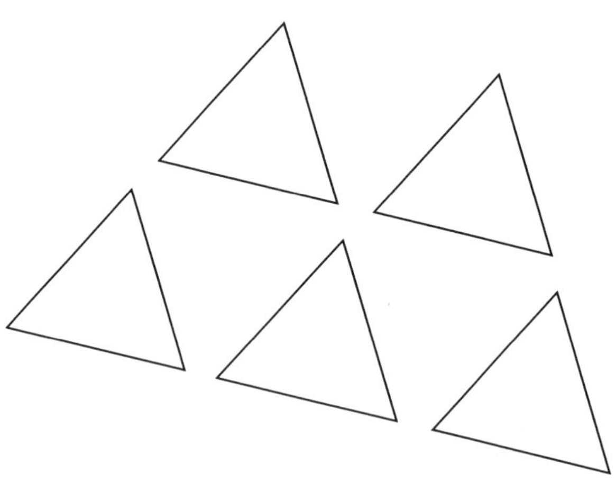

Directions Have children color the groups of 4 triangles red and the groups of 5 triangles yellow.

Name ______________________________

Reading and Writing 4 and 5

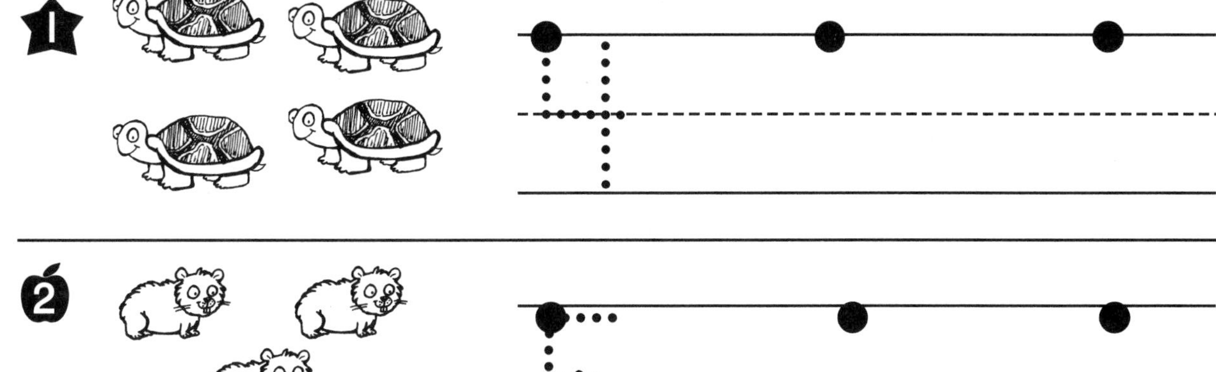

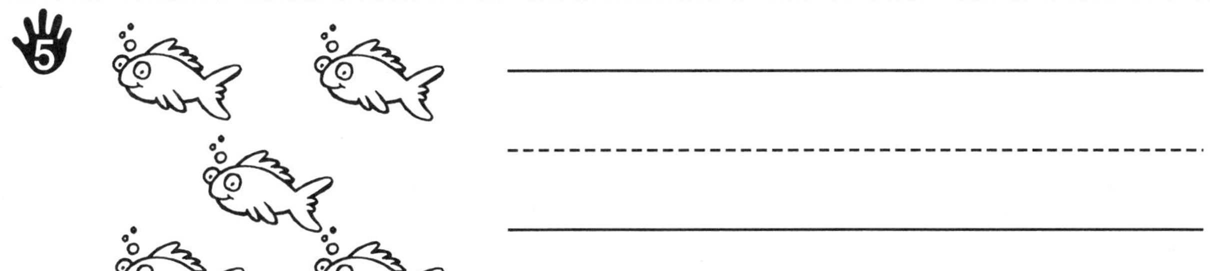

Directions Have children count each group and practice writing the number.

Name ____________________

Reading and Writing 0

P 3-5

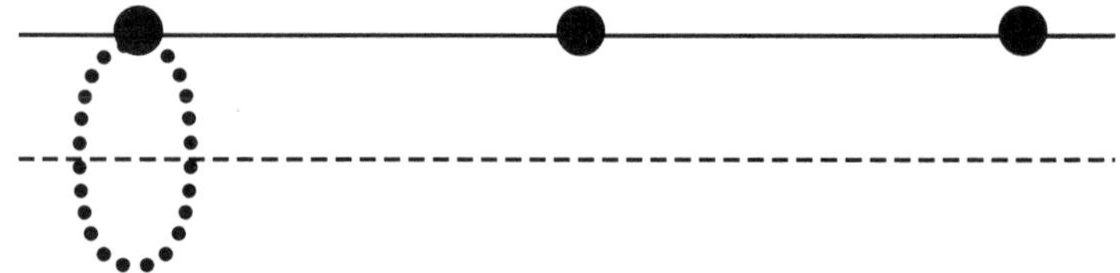

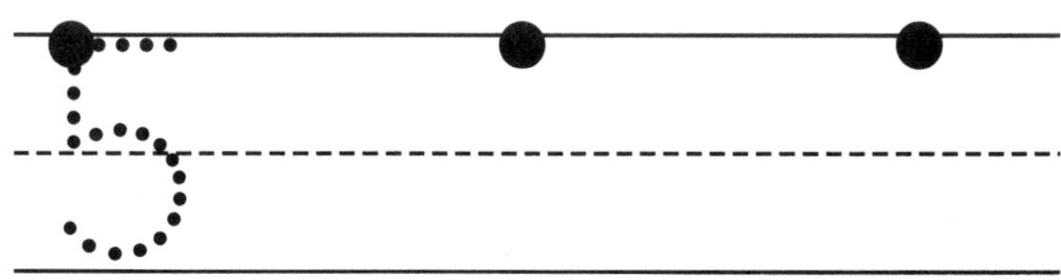

Directions Have children count each group and practice writing the number.

Name ______________________________

Comparing Numbers Through 5

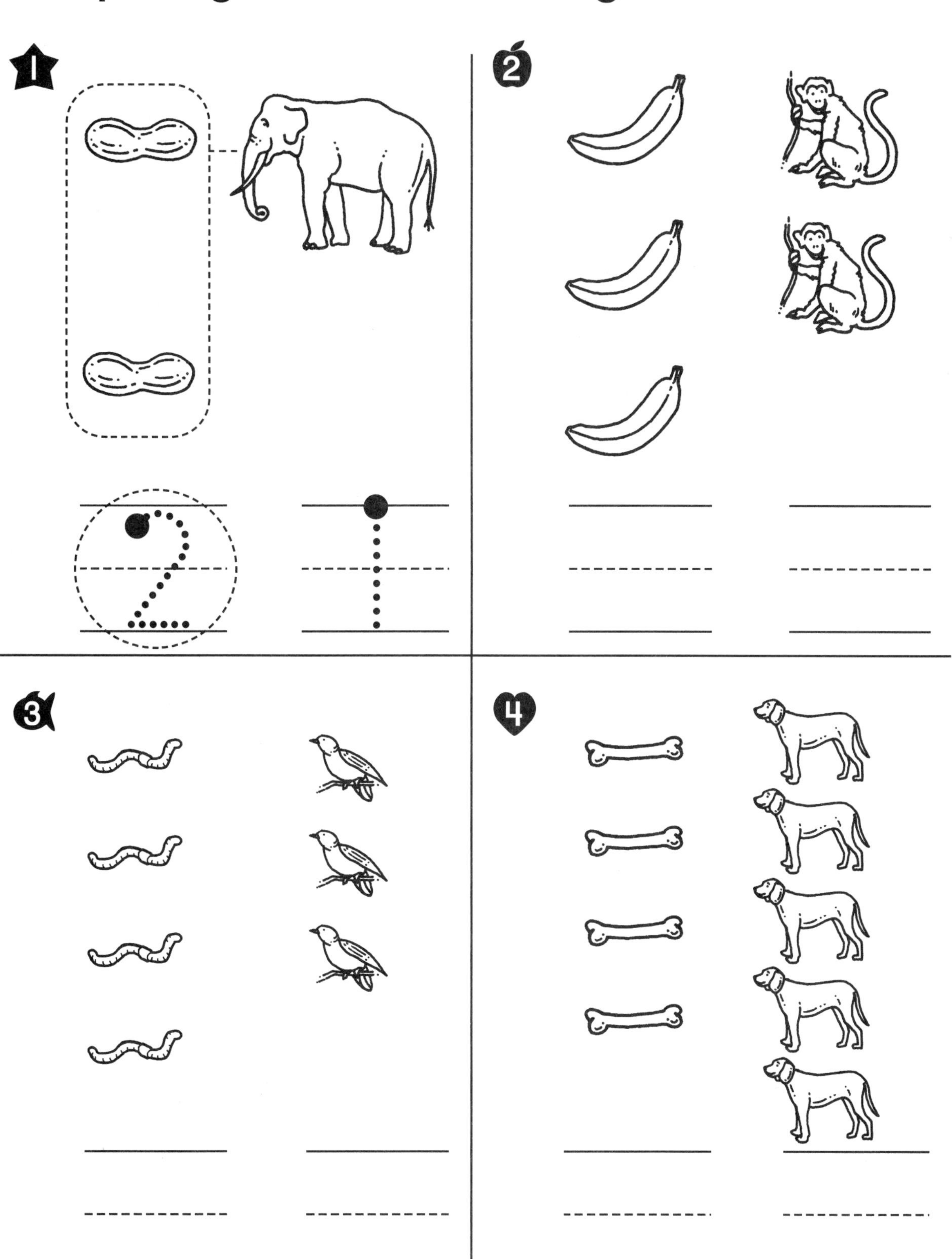

Directions Exercises 1–2: Have children draw a line from each item in one group to an item in the other group and circle the group that has more. Then have children count the items, write the corresponding numbers, and circle the number that is more. Exercises 3–4: Repeat for items that are fewer and circle the groups and numbers that are less.

Name ______________________________

Ordering Numbers 0 Through 5

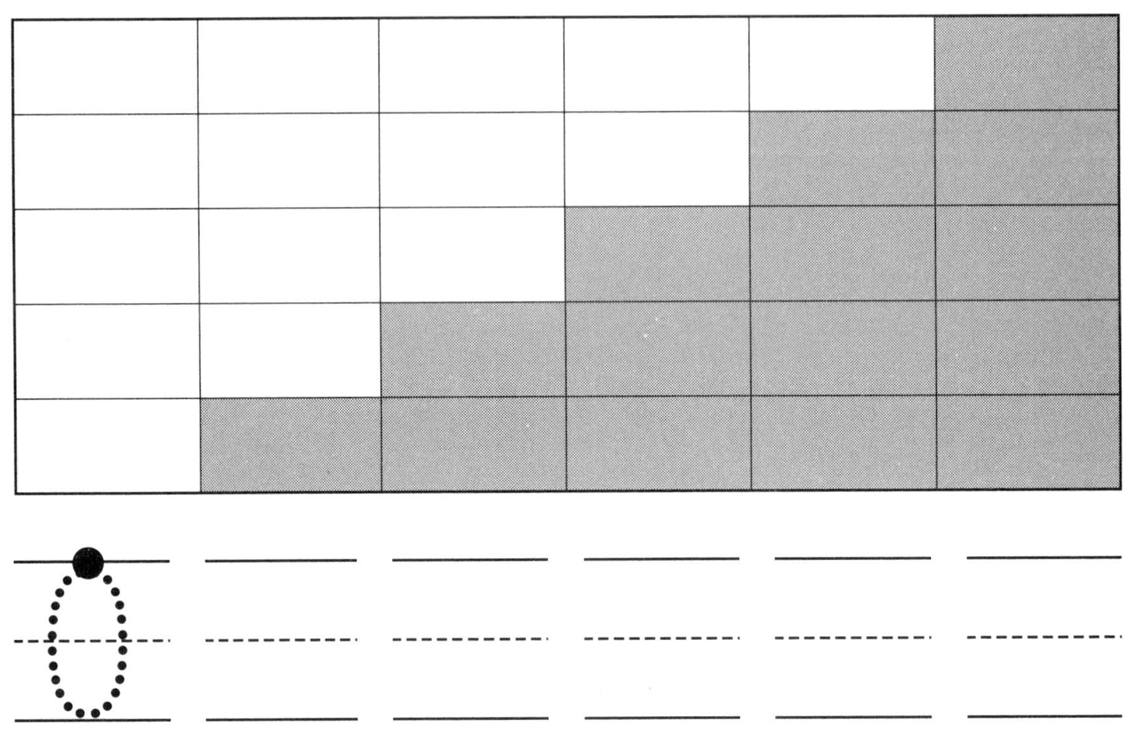

0

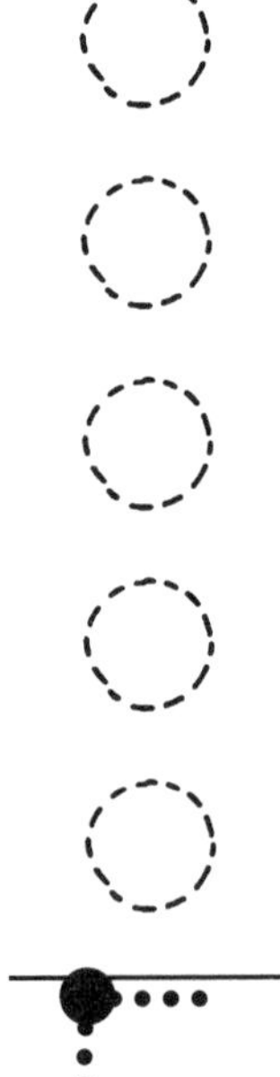

5 _ 3 _ 1 0

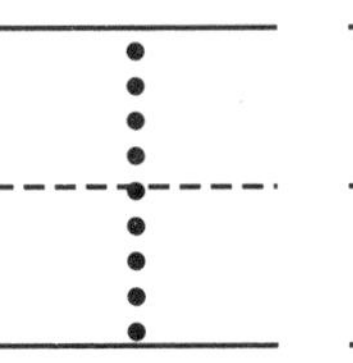

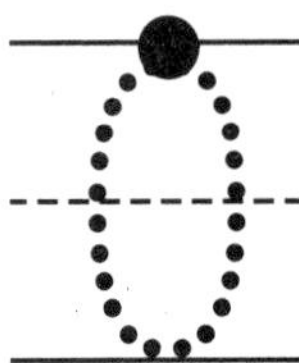

Directions Exercise 1: Have children write numbers to show the number of squares shaded and 0–5 in order. Exercise 2: Have children tell a story about eating crackers one at a time until zero are left. Have children show what happens by drawing the crackers in order and writing the missing numbers.

Name ______________________________

Make a Graph

Making the Fewest

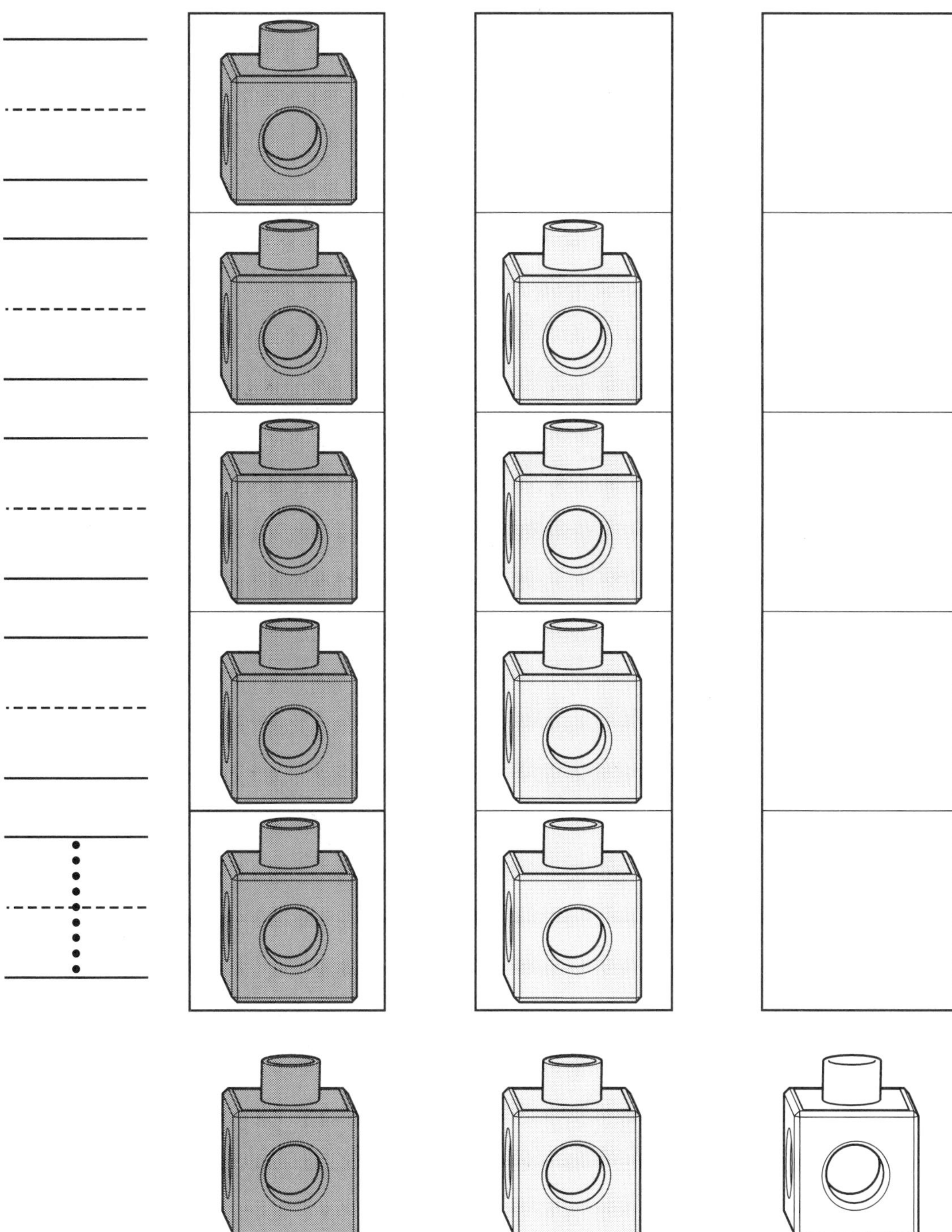

Directions In Column 3 have children use cubes to show a group with the fewest cubes. Then have children draw pictures of the cubes in the squares. To complete the graph, have children write the numbers 1–5 up the left side.

Name ____________________

Ordinal Numbers Through Fifth

P 3-9

Directions Have children circle the first elephant in Exercise 1, the second elephant in Exercise 2, the third elephant in Exercise 3, the fourth elephant in Exercise 4, the fifth elephant in Exercise 5. Check that children understand where each line begins and ends.

Name ____________________

Mix and Match

1 ______

2 ______

Directions Ask children to name things you can use on a rainy day and things you can use on a sunny day. Exercise 1: Have children count the rainy day items and write the number. Exercise 2: Have children count the sunny day items and write the number. Then have children circle the number that is less.

Name ______________________________

Counting 6 and 7

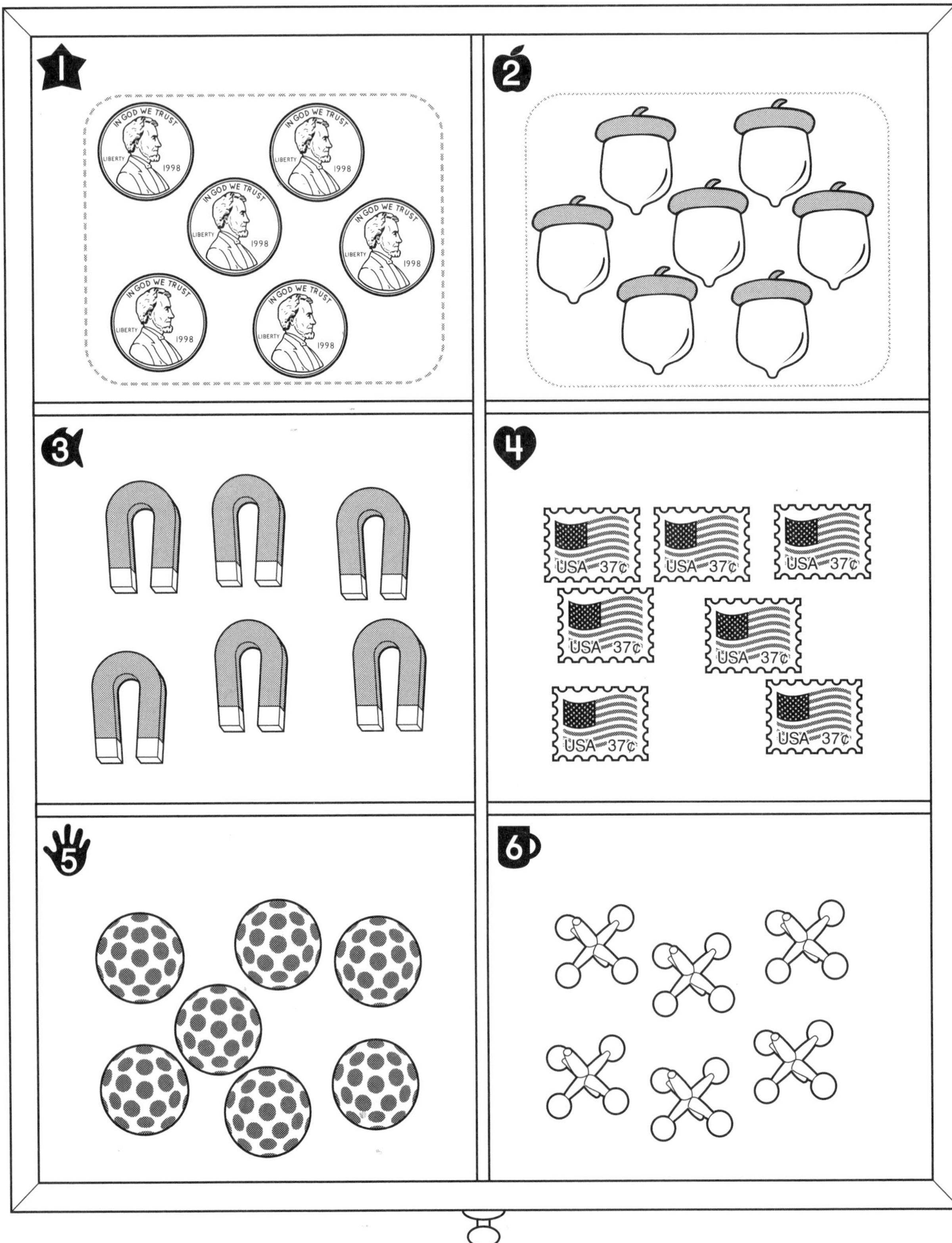

Directions Ask children to count the groups. Have them use a green crayon to circle each group of 6 and a purple crayon to circle each group of 7.

Name ______________________________

Counting 8

P 4-2

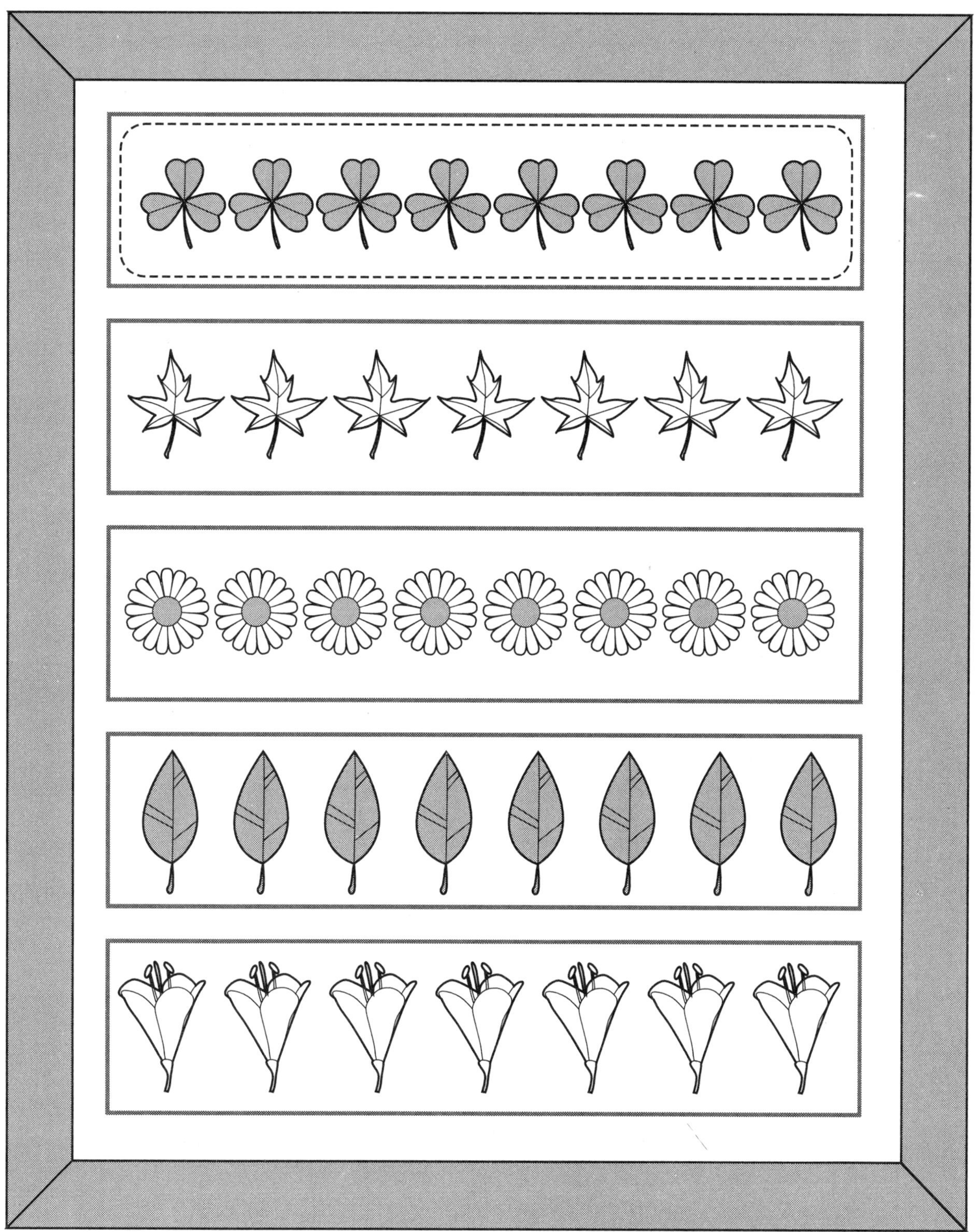

Directions Ask children to count the groups. Have them circle each group of 8.

Name ____________________

Reading and Writing 6, 7, and 8

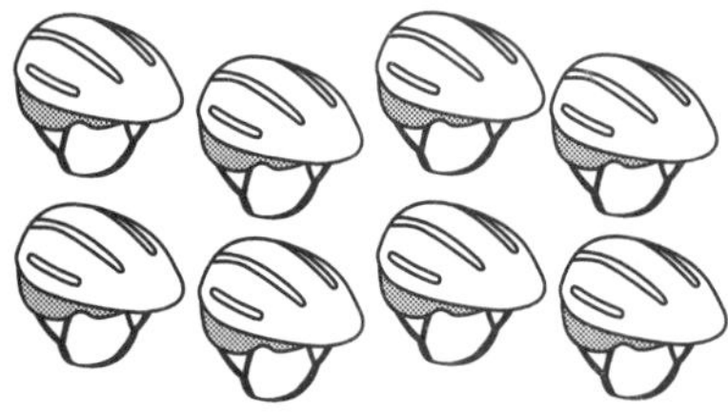

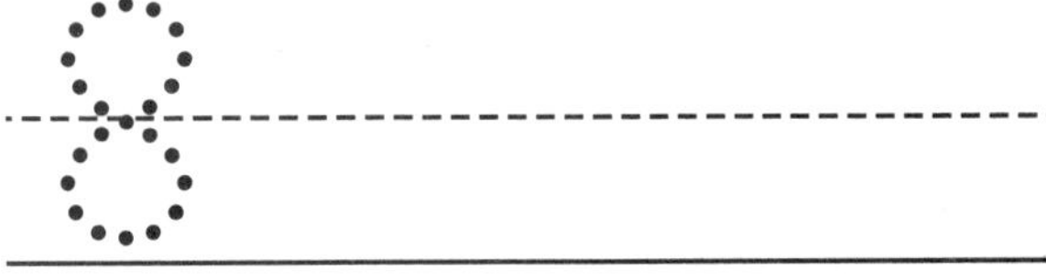

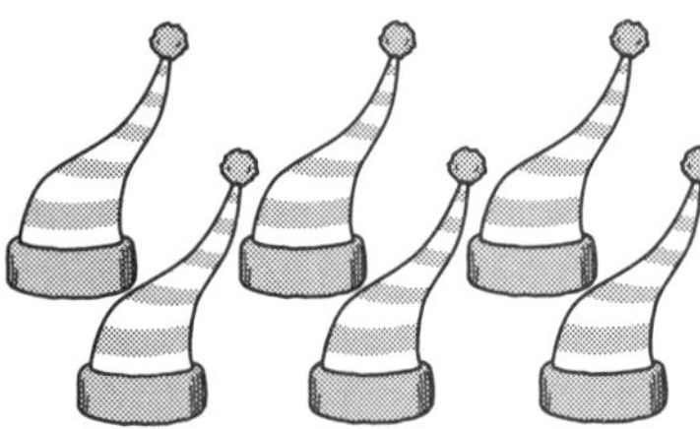

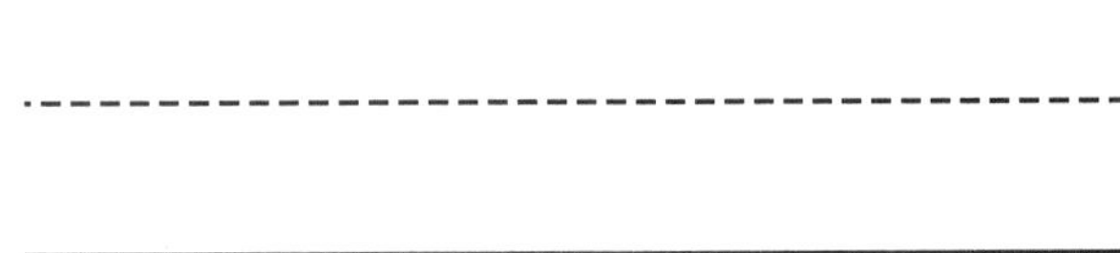

Directions Have children count each group and practice writing the number.

Name ____________________

Counting 9 and 10

P 4-4

Directions Ask children to count the groups. Have them use a green crayon to circle each group of 9 and an orange crayon to circle each group of 10.

Name ___________________________

Reading and Writing 9 and 10

P 4-5

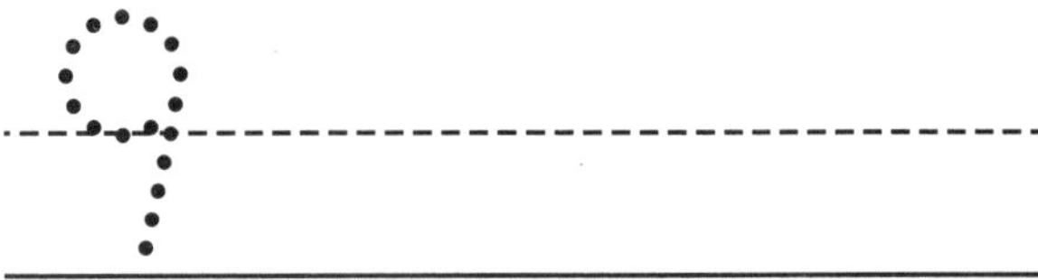

2

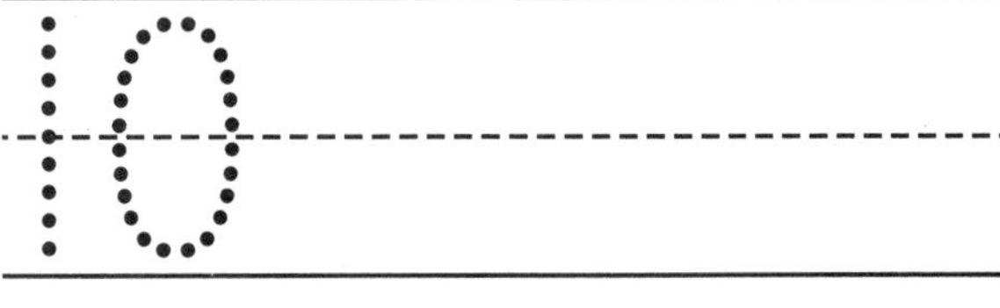

3

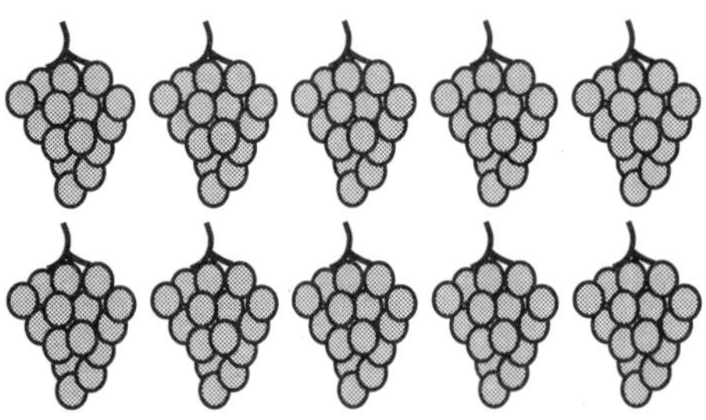

4

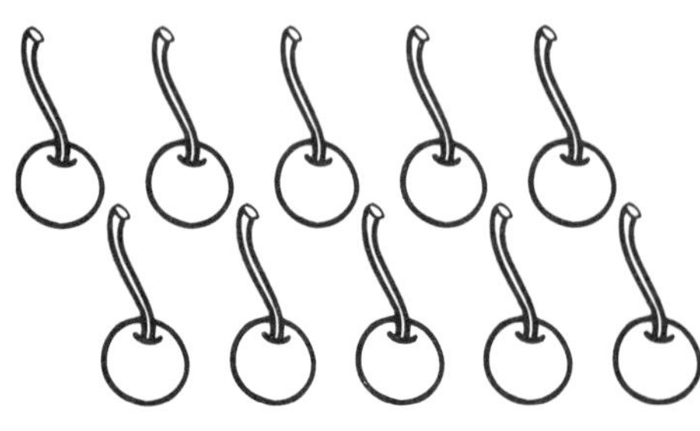

Directions Have children count each group and practice writing the number.

Name ____________________

Comparing Numbers Through 10

1

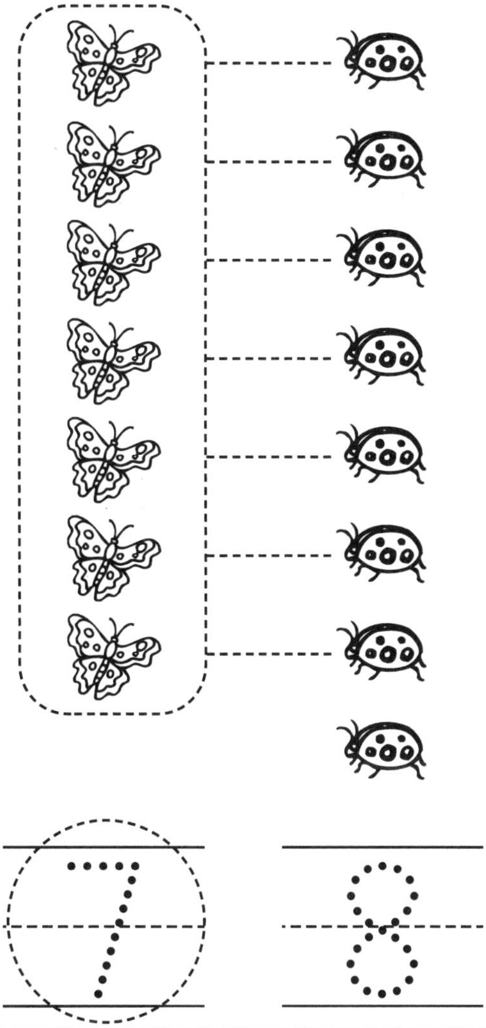

7 8

2

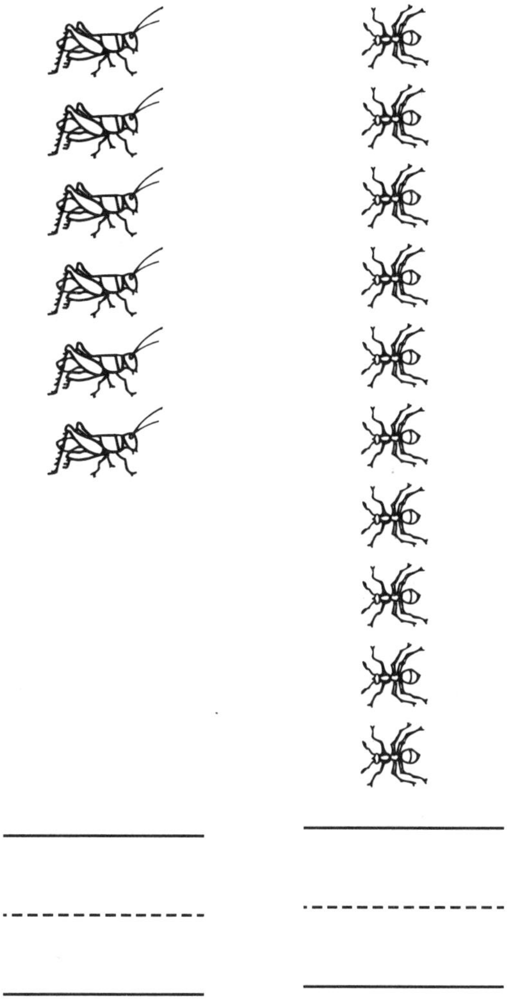

3

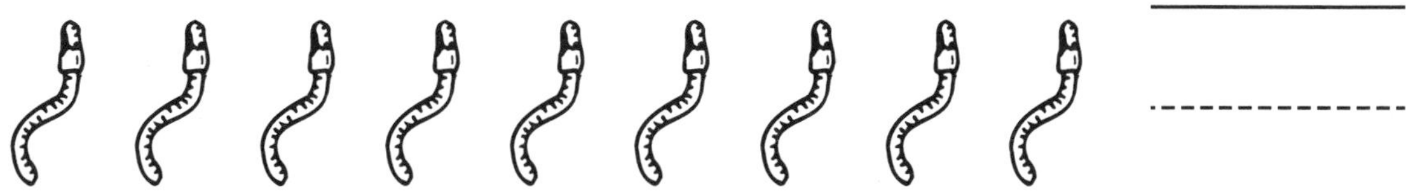

Directions Have children draw a line from each item in one group to an item in the other group and circle the group that has fewer. Then have children count the items, write the corresponding numbers, and circle the lesser number.

Name ____________________

Comparing Numbers to 5 and 10

P 4-7

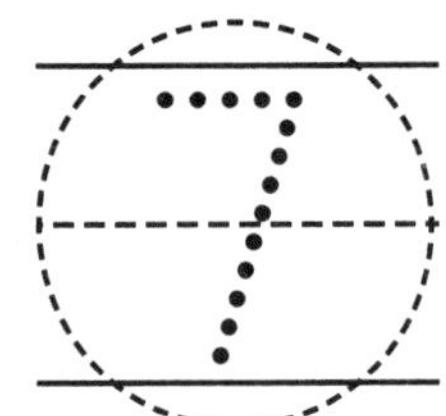
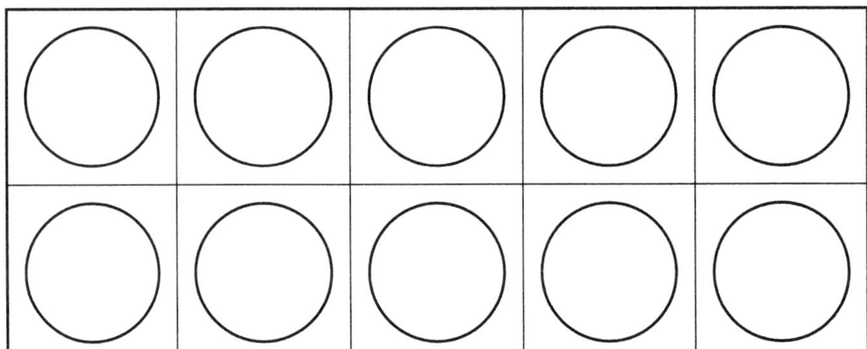

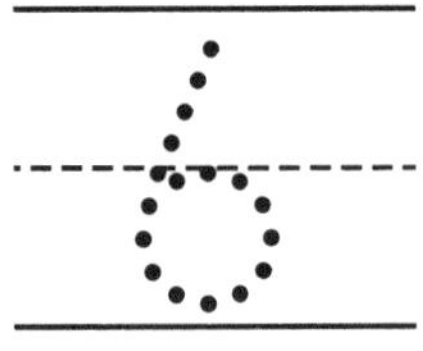
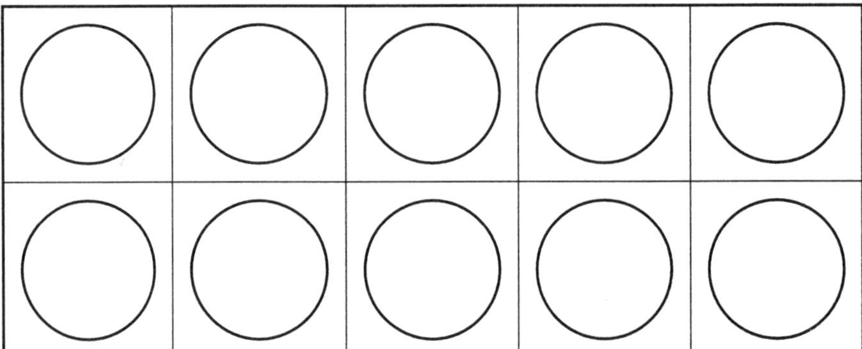

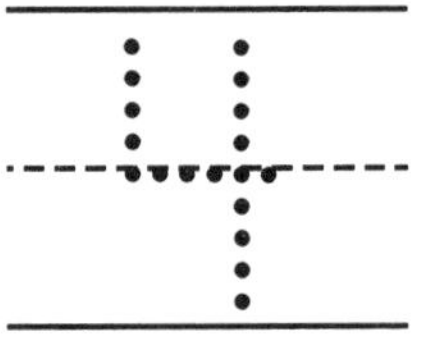
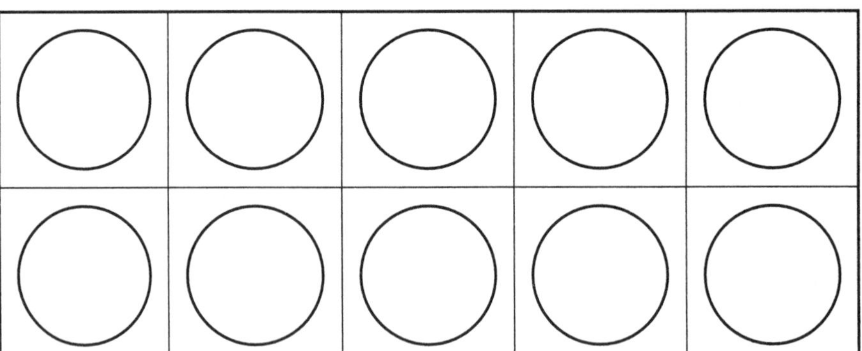

Directions Have children trace each number and color counter outlines to show that number. Then have children circle the numbers that are more than 5 but less than 10.

Name ______________________________

Ordering Numbers 0 Through 10

P 4-8

0
1
2
3
4
5
6
7
8
9
10

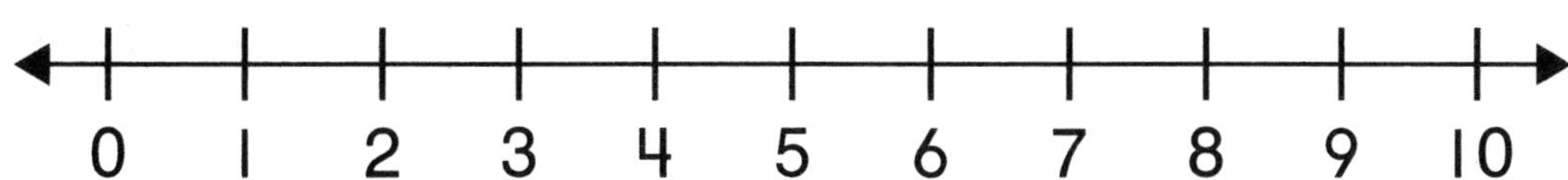

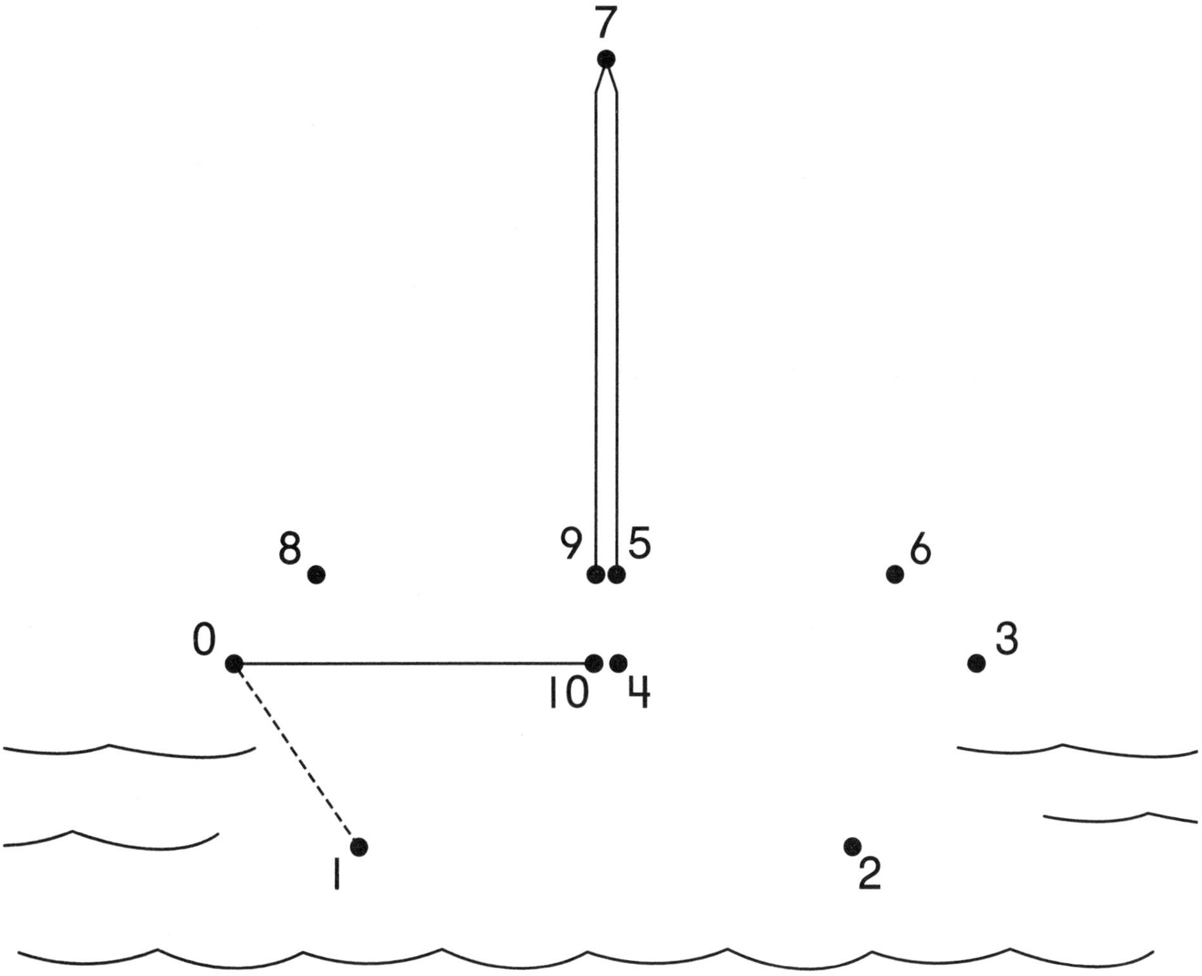

7
8
9
5
6
0
3
10
4
1
2

Directions Have children use the numbers in the number line to connect the dots on the page.

Name ____________________

Ordinal Numbers Through Tenth

P 4-9

2

3

4

5

Directions Have children circle the fifth dog, the sixth mouse, the seventh chick, the eighth cat, and the tenth rabbit.

Name ____________________

PROBLEM-SOLVING STRATEGY **P 4-10**

Look for a Pattern

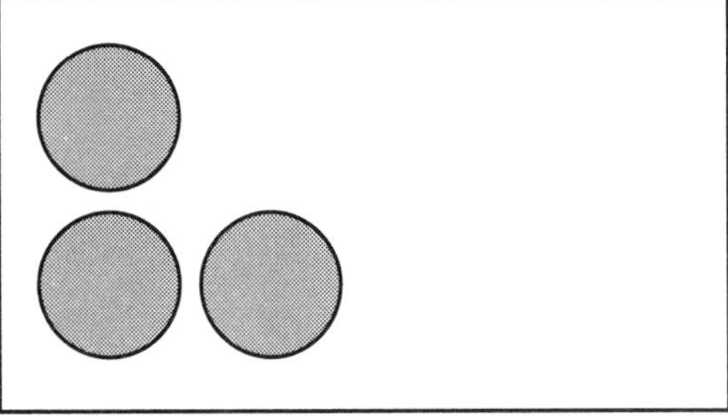

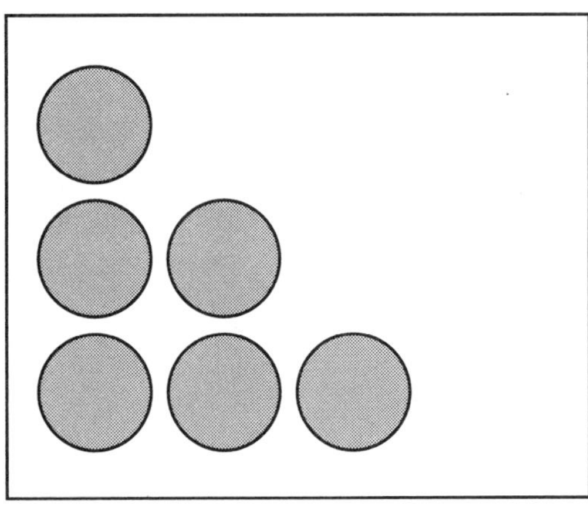

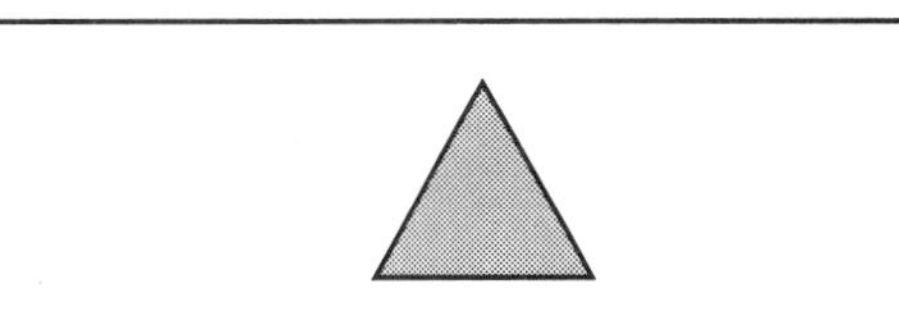

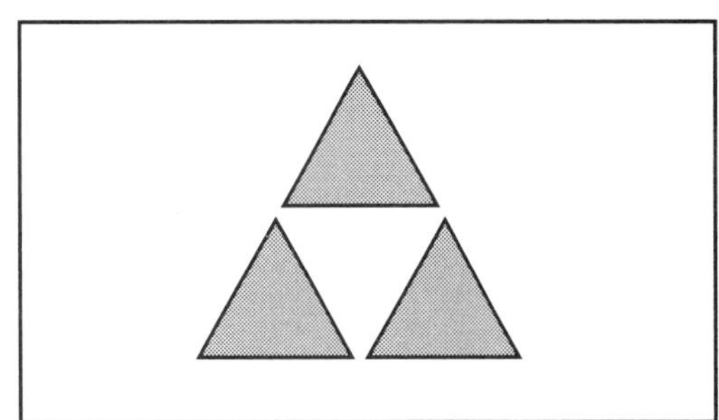

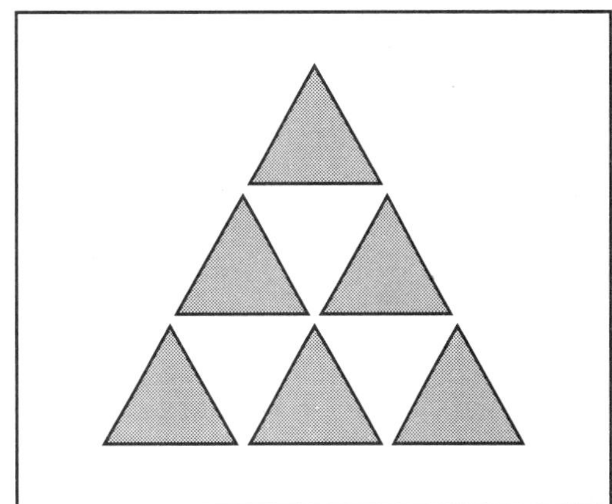

Directions Have children identify how the patterns grow and draw shapes to continue the patterns.

Name ______________________________

PROBLEM-SOLVING APPLICATIONS **P 4-11**

Let's Have a Picnic

Directions Tell children that camels can have one or two humps. Have children find the third camel and tell what it looks like. Then have children circle the third camel. Repeat for the fifth, eighth, and ninth camels.

Name ____________________

Counting 11-20

P 5-1

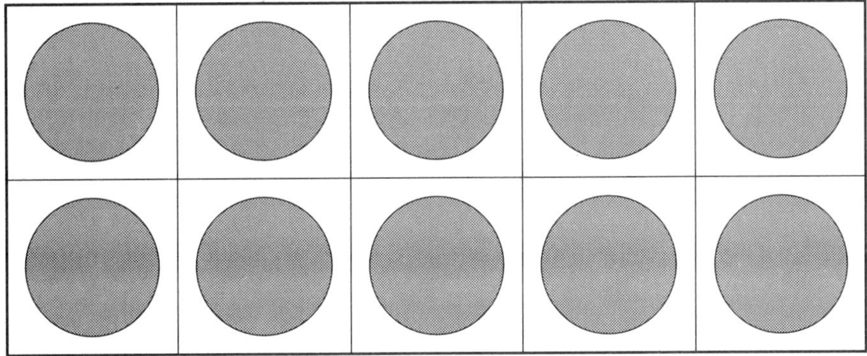

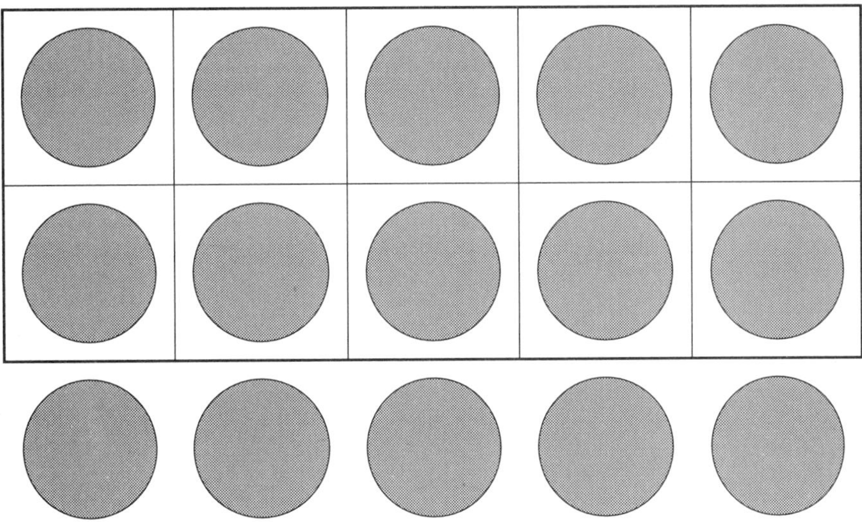

Directions Exercise 1: Have children choose a number from 11 through 15 and use counters to count and model the number. Then have children draw and color enough extra counters to show the number. Exercise 2: Have children repeat for a number from 16 through 20.

Name ______________________________

Reading and Writing 11 and 12

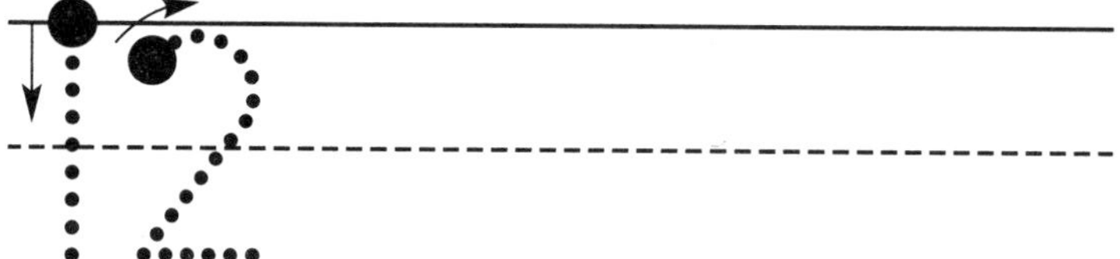

Directions Have children count each group and practice writing the numbers.

Name ______________________________

Reading and Writing 13, 14, and 15

P 5-3

1  13

2  14

3  15

4

5

Directions Have children count each group and practice writing the numbers.

Name ______________________________

Reading and Writing 16 and 17

1

16

2

17

3

4

Directions Have children count each group and write the numbers.

Name ____________________

Reading and Writing 18, 19, and 20

P 5-5

1 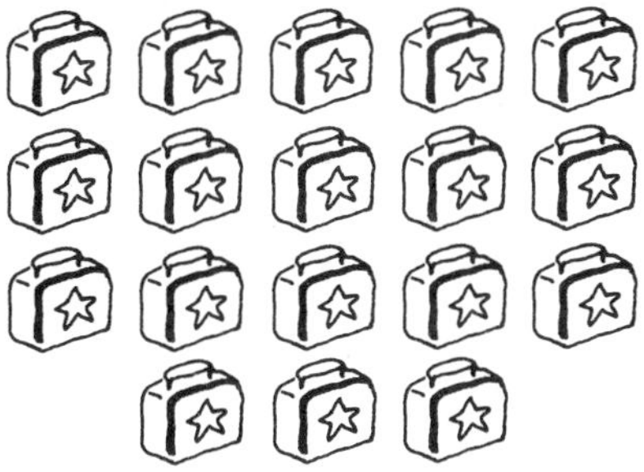 18

2 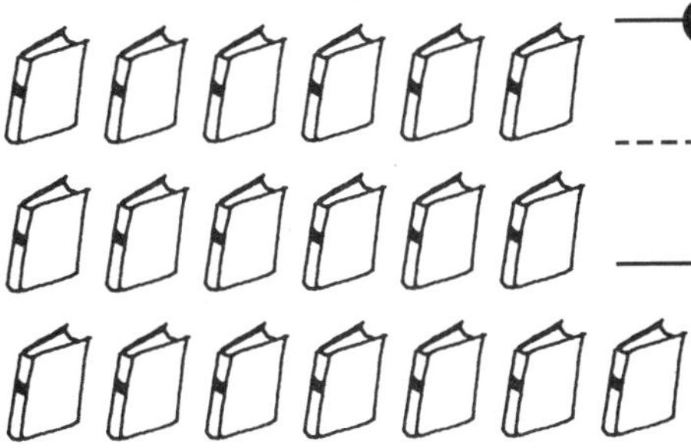 19

3 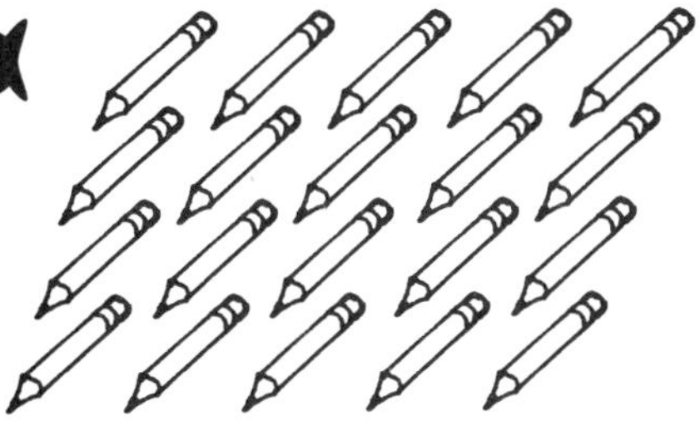 20

4

5

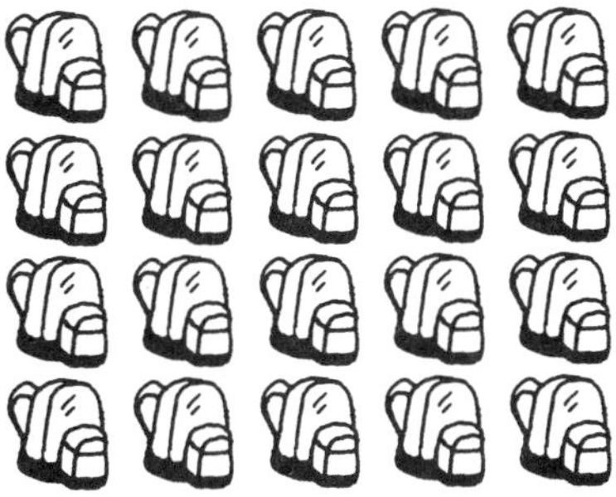

Directions Have children count each group and practice writing the numbers.

Name ___________________________

Skip Counting by 2s and 5s

P 5-6

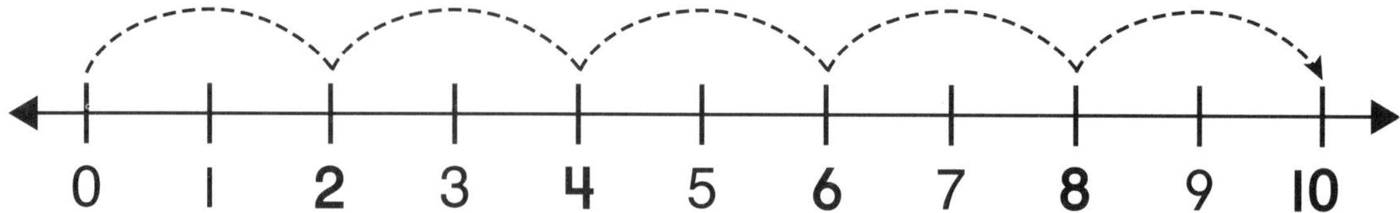

2 ______ ______ ______ ______

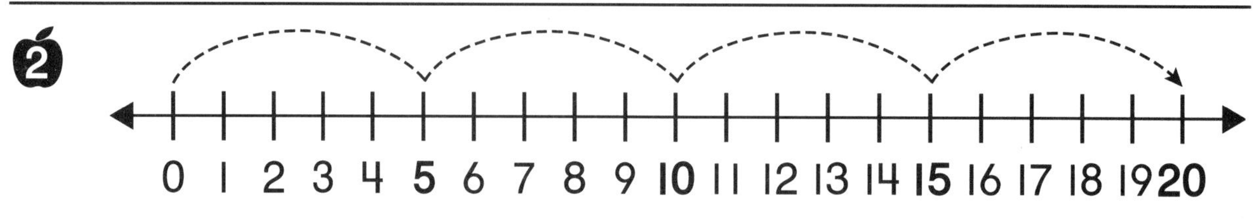

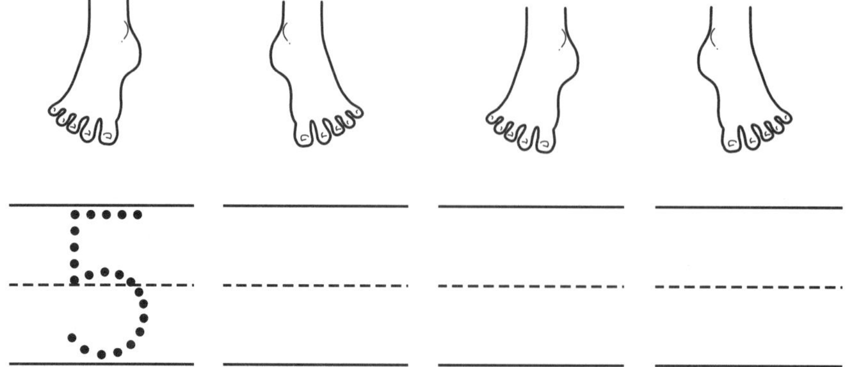

5 ______ ______ ______

Directions Exercise 1: Have children skip count by 2s to count the rabbits and record the numbers. Exercise 2: Have children skip count by 5s to count the toes and record the numbers.

Name ______________________

Counting to 31

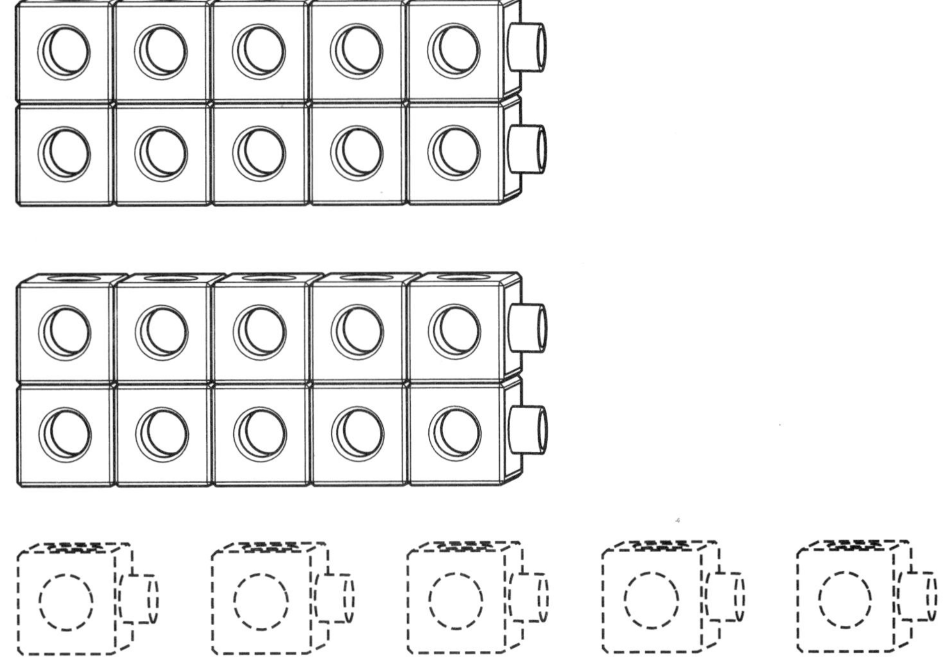

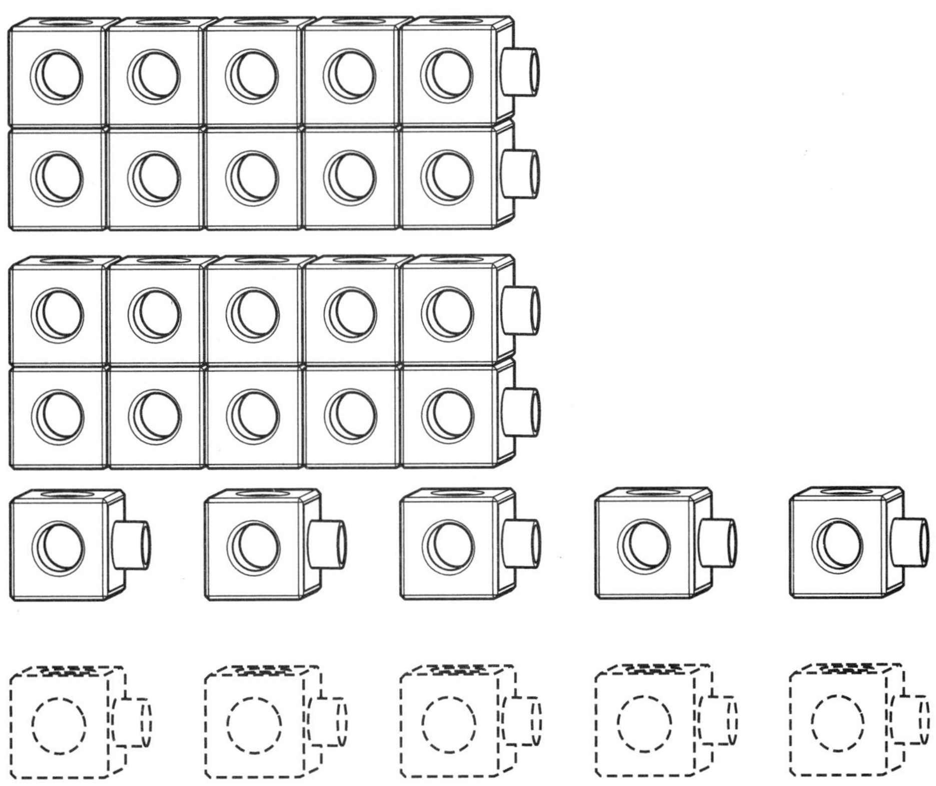

Directions Exercise 1: Have children choose a number from 21 through 25 and use cubes to count and model the number. Then have them draw and color enough extra cubes to show the number. Exercise 2: Have children repeat for a number from 26 through 30.

Name ___

Reading and Writing Numbers Through 31

P 5-8

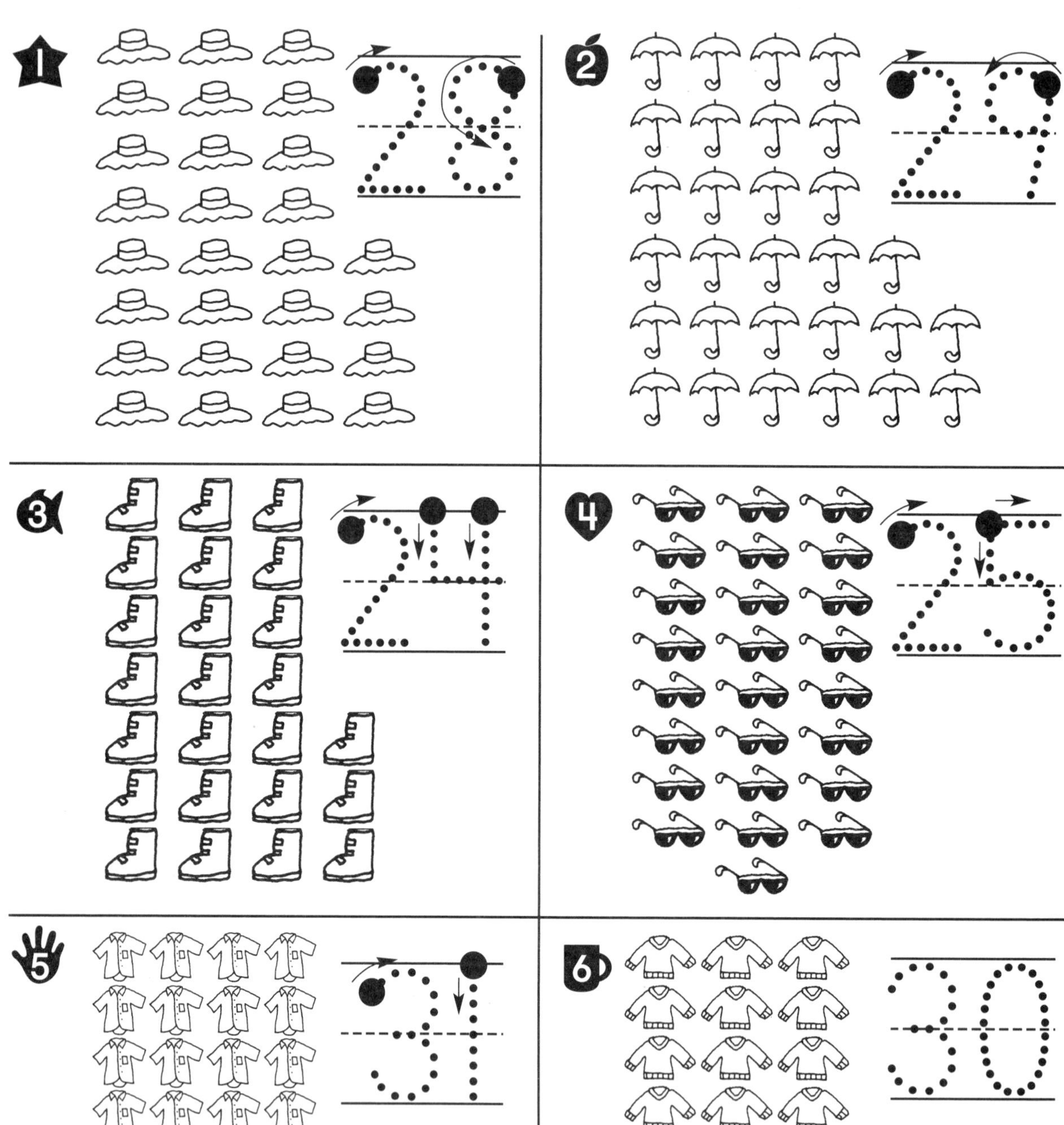

Directions For each exercise have children count the objects and write the number.

Name ______________________________

Using Estimation

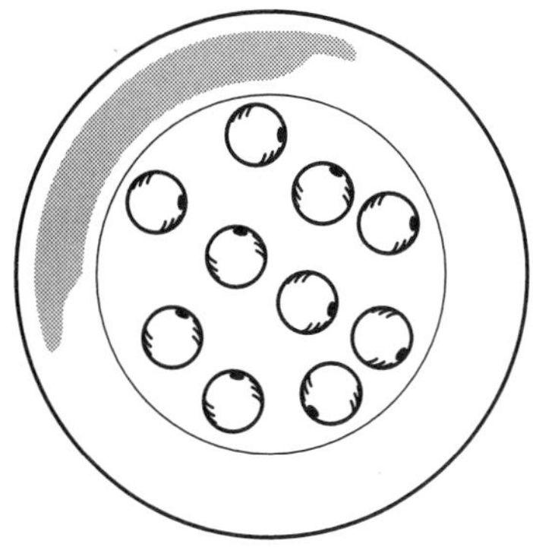

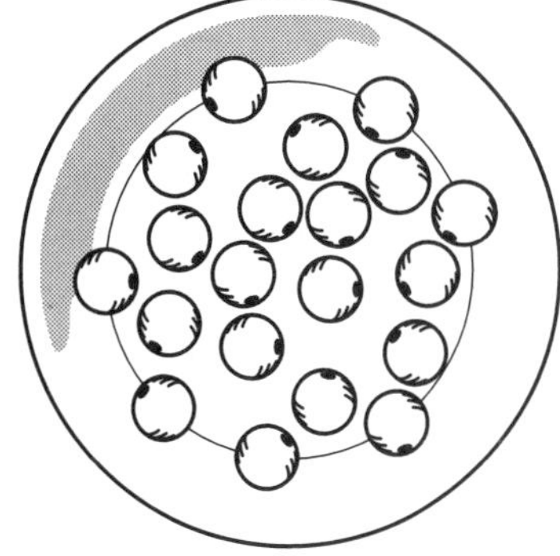

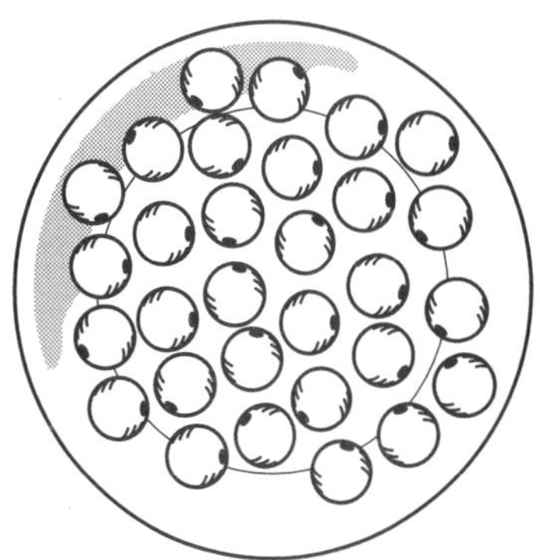

10

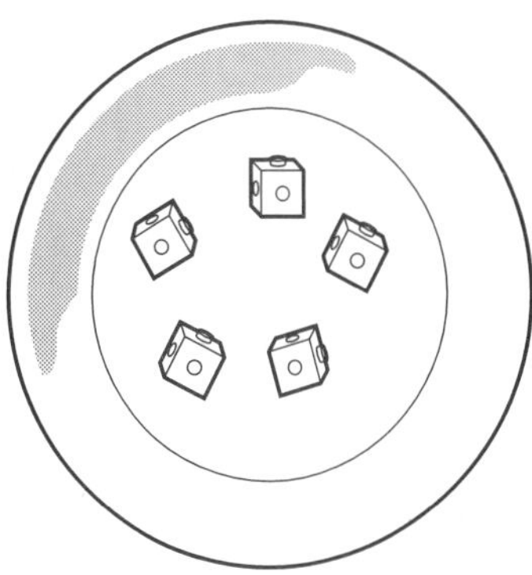

20

30

Directions Exercise 1: Have children circle the plate with about 30 beads on it. Exercise 2: Have children circle the plate with about 5 cubes on it. Exercise 3: Have children circle the plate with about 20 teddy bear counters on it.

Name ______________________________

Comparing Numbers Through 31

P 5-10

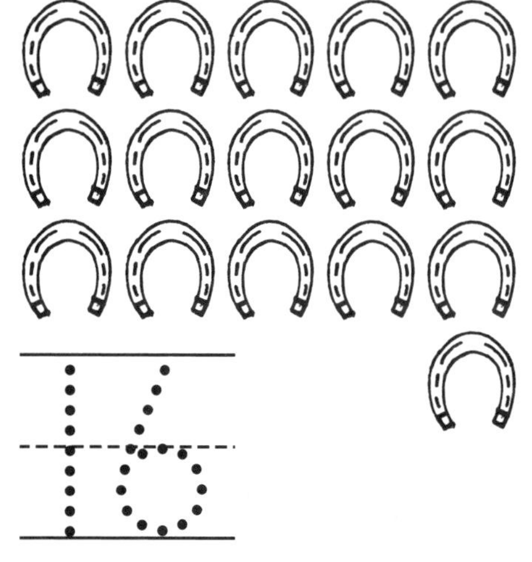

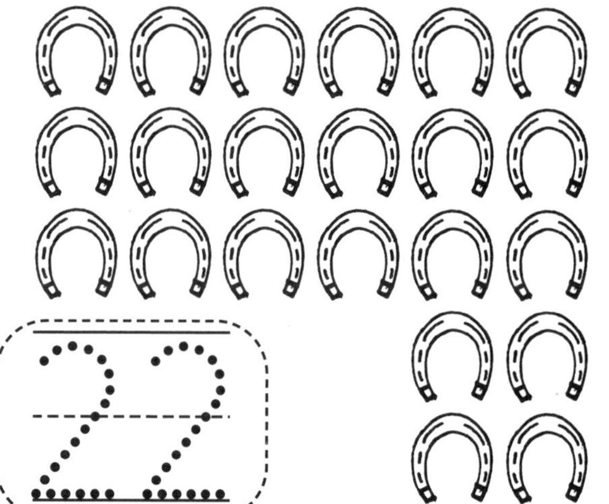

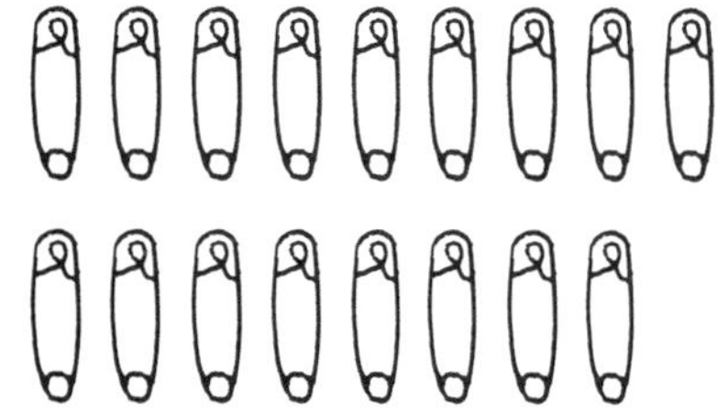

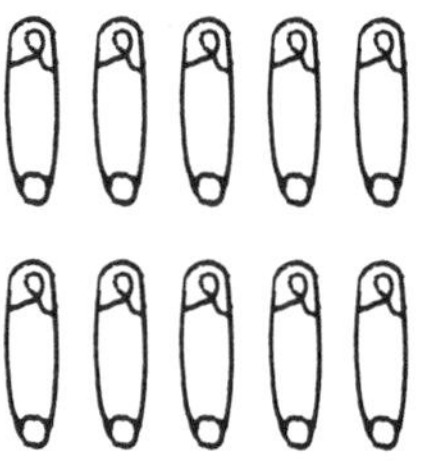

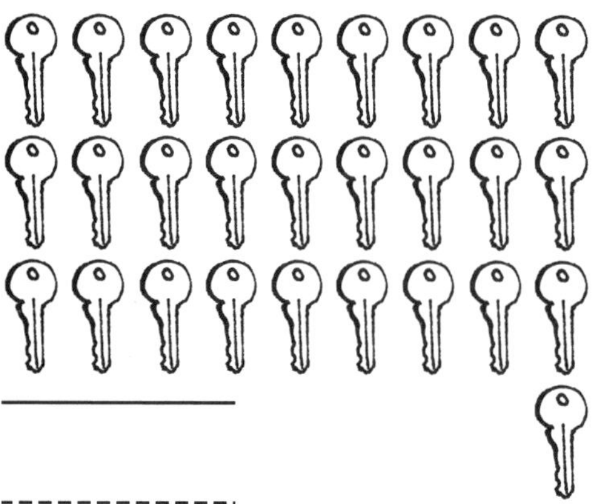

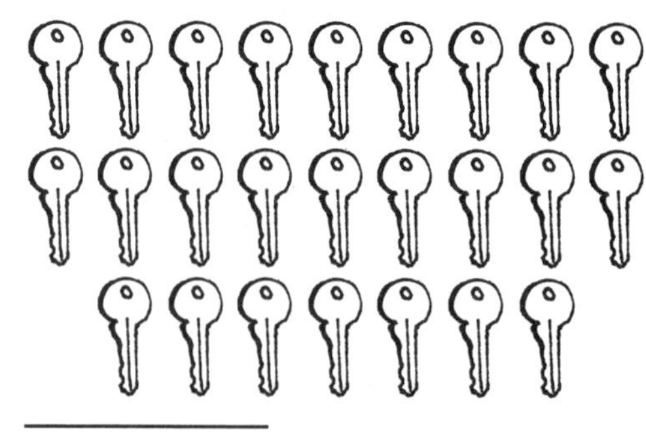

Directions For each exercise have children count the groups of objects, write the numbers, and circle the greater number.

Name ______________________________

Numbers on a Calendar

P 5-11

June

Sunday	Monday	Tuesday	Wednesday	Thursday	Friday	Saturday
	1	2	3	4	5	6
7	8	9	___	11	___	13
14	15	___	17	___	19	20
21	22	23	24	___	26	27
28	___	30				

Directions Have children write the numbers that come before and after 5, 11, and 17. Then have children write the numbers that come between 21 and 23, 24 and 26, and 28 and 30.

Name ______________________________

PROBLEM-SOLVING STRATEGY **P 5-12**

Make a Table

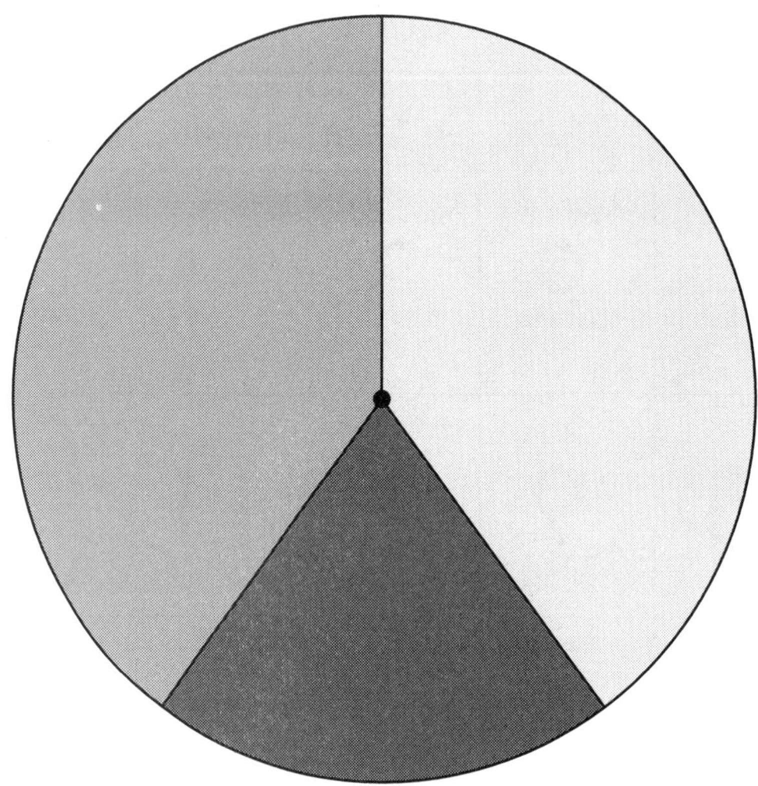

Color Tally

(dark gray)	
(medium gray)	
(light gray)	

Directions Have children place a paper clip on the spinner and hold it in place with a pencil. (Point of pencil should be on the black dot.) Ask children to make a tally mark in the table after each of 10 spins.

Name ______________________________

A World of Bugs

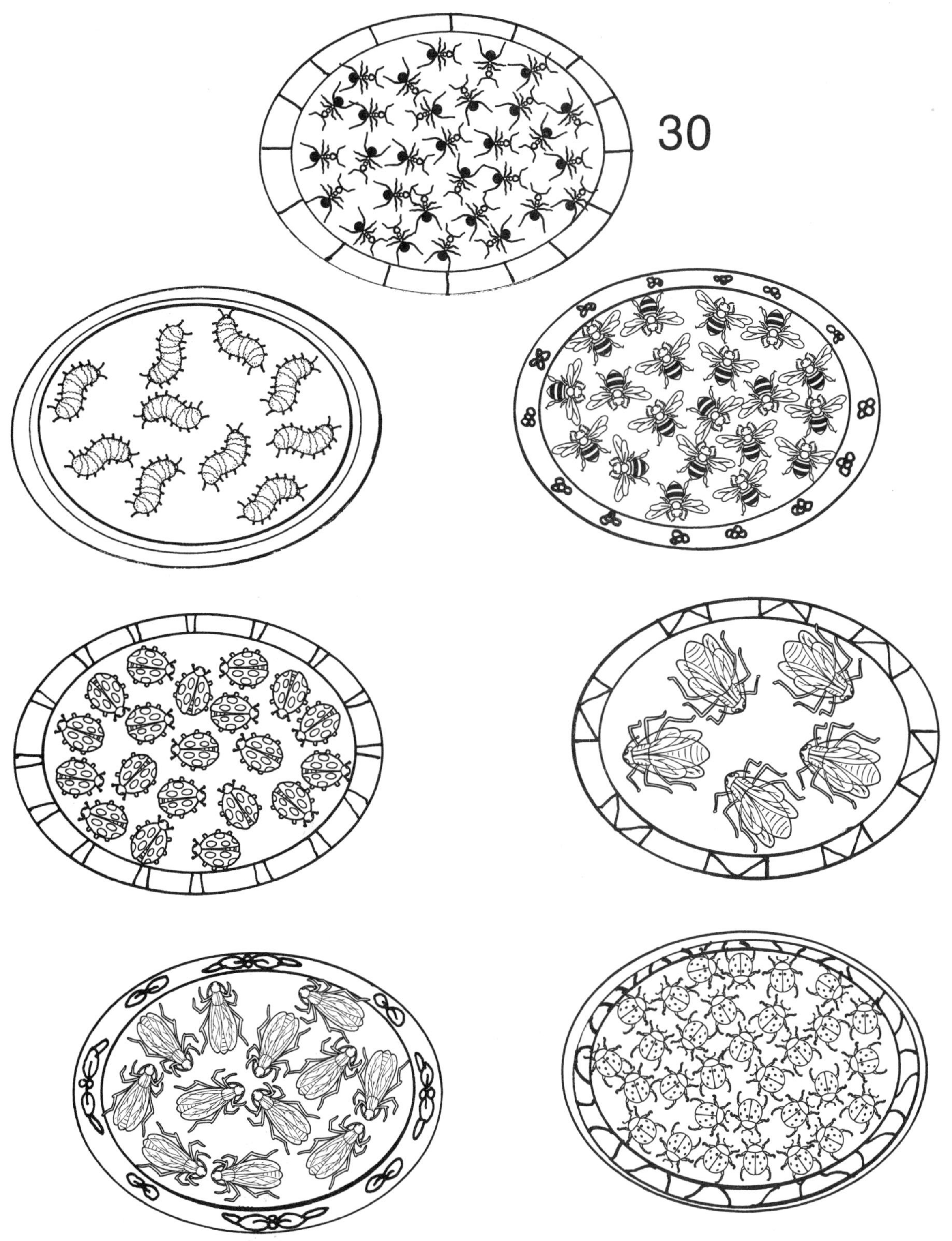

Directions Ask children how many bugs are on the top plate. Then have children look at the other groups and estimate which plates have about 20 bugs. Have them circle these plates.

Name ______________________________

Comparing and Ordering by Size

P 6-1

2

3

4

Directions Have children order the houses in each exercise by circling the largest one, marking an *X* on the smallest one, and underlining the medium-sized one.

Name ________________________________

Comparing by Length

P 6-2

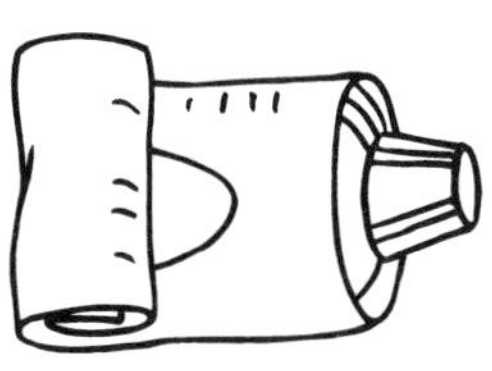

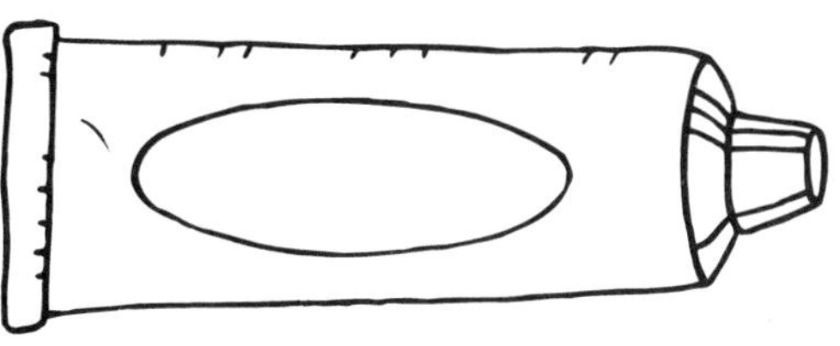

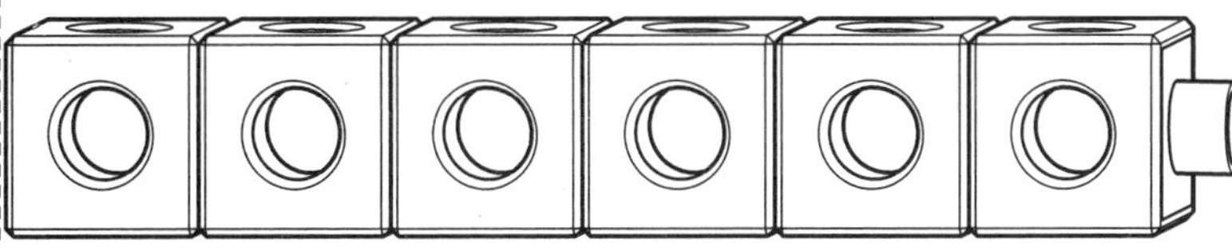

Directions Exercise 1: Have children circle the longer tube of toothpaste and mark an *X* on the shorter tube. Exercise 2: Have children circle the taller candle and mark an *X* on the shorter candle. Exercise 3: Have children draw one or more objects that are longer than the cube train.

Name ______________________________

Ordering by Length

P 6-3

Directions Have children put the flowers in order by coloring the tallest green and the shortest yellow.

Name ______________________

Measuring Length

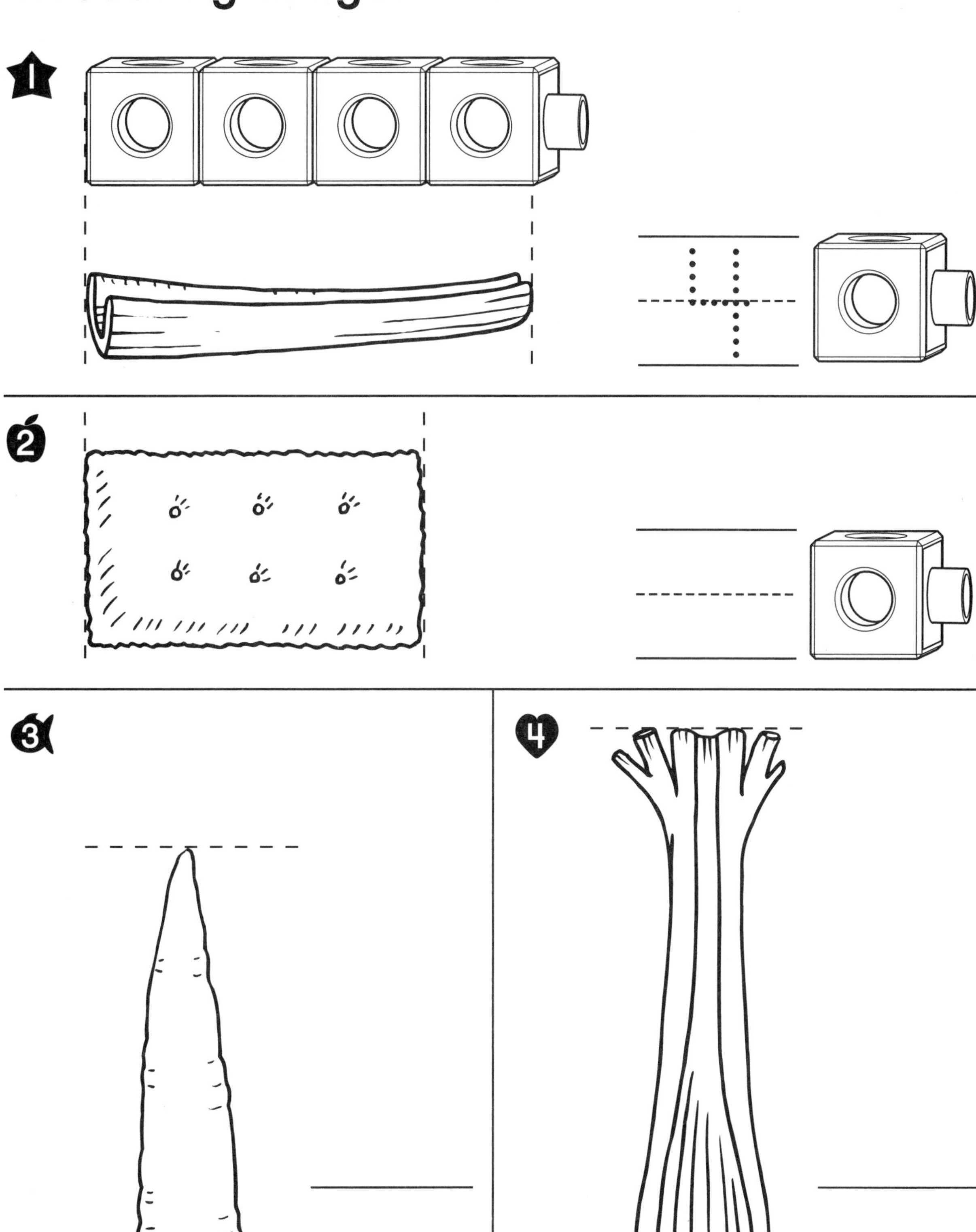

Directions Exercises 1–2: Have children use cubes to measure the length of each object and record the number of cubes. Exercises 3–4: Have children use cubes to measure the height of each object and record the number of cubes.

Name ______________________________

Estimating and Measuring Length

P 6-5

Estimate		Measure
1		
2		
3		
4		

Directions Have children estimate and record the length of each classroom object in paper clips. Then have children measure and record the actual length.

Name ________________________________

PROBLEM-SOLVING STRATEGY **P 6-6**

Try, Check, and Revise

Estimate		Measure
1 ______ ______ ______		______ ______ ______
2 ______ ______ ______		______ ______ ______
3 ______ ______ ______		______ ______ ______

Directions For each exercise have children estimate the number of tiles they will need to cover the shape and record the number. Then have children cover the shape with tiles and record the number used.

Name ______________________________

Comparing and Ordering by Capacity

P 6-7

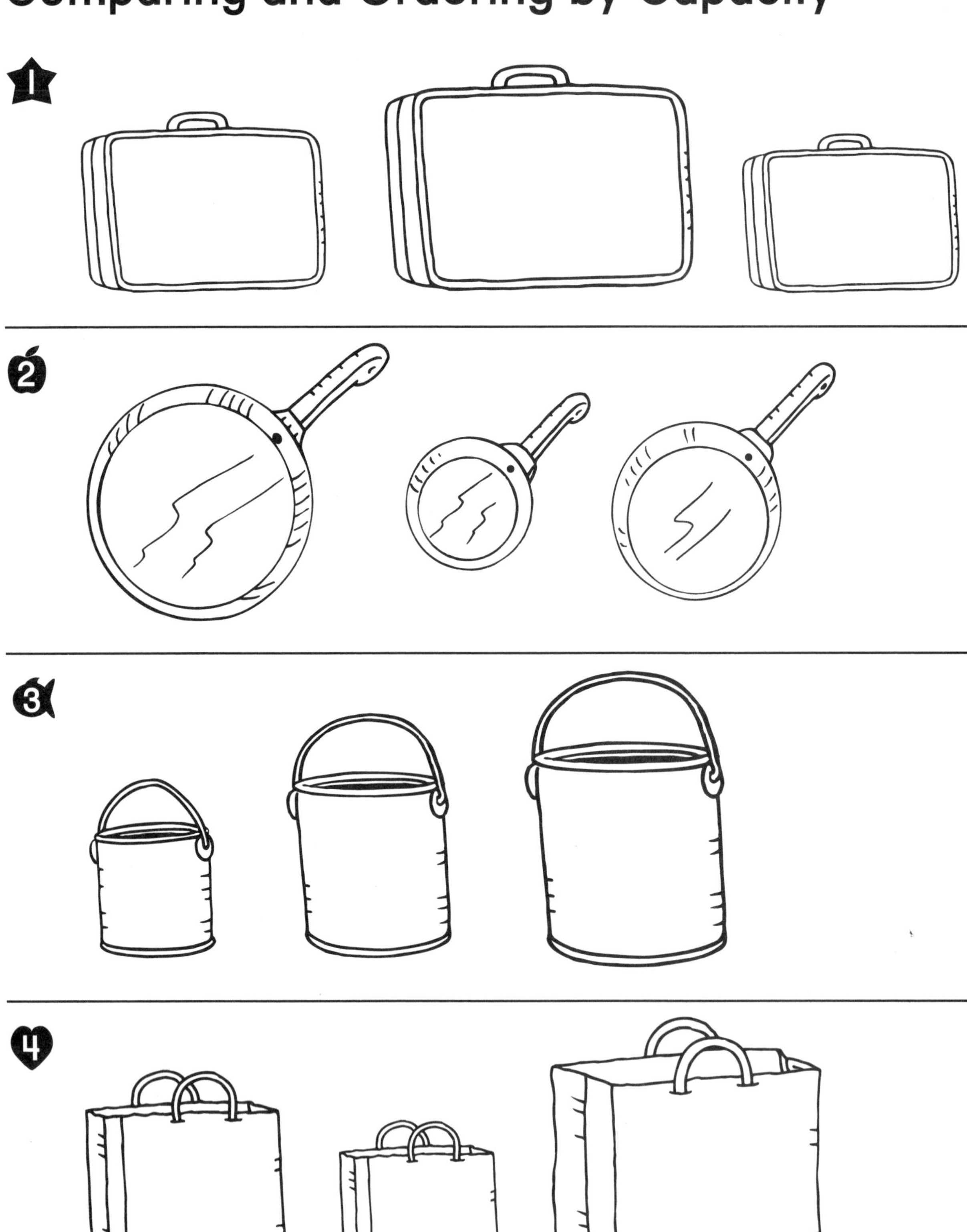

Directions Have children order the containers in each exercise by coloring the one that can hold the most green and the one that can hold the least yellow.

Name ______________________________

Estimating and Measuring Capacity

P 6-8

Estimate		Measure
1 6	6 5 7 4 3 1 2	7
2		
3		
4		

Directions Use a container like the one pictured. Have children estimate how many cubes would fill each container to the line shown and record the number. Then have children fill each container with cubes to the line shown and record the number used.

Name ______________________________

Comparing and Ordering by Weight

P 6-9

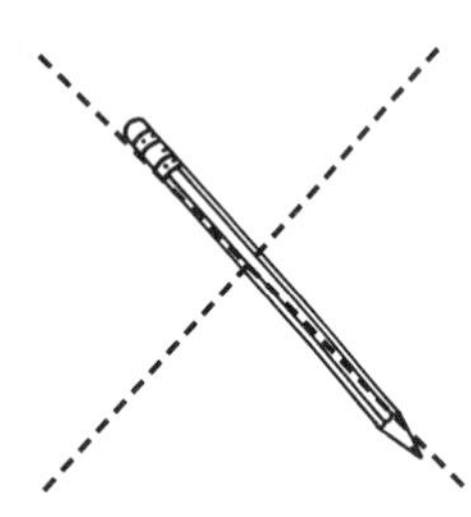

2

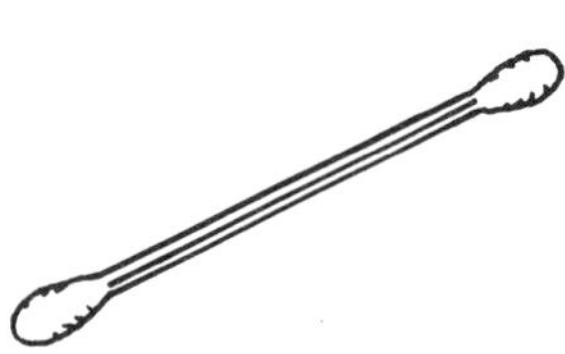

3

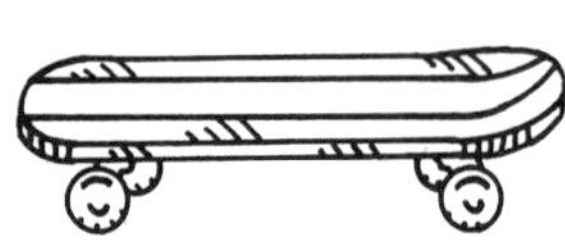

4

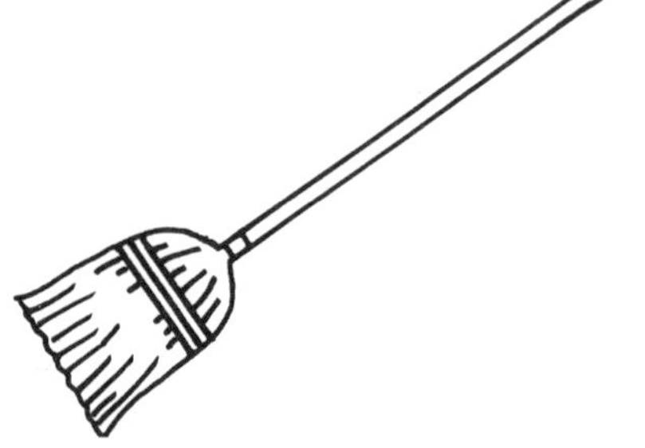

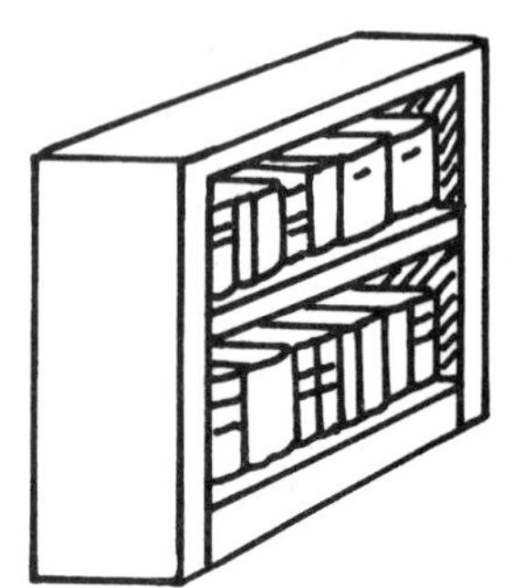

Directions Have children order the objects in each exercise by circling the heaviest object and marking an X on the lightest object.

Name ____________________

Estimating and Measuring Weight

P 6-10

Estimate		Measure
1 ______		______
2 ______	Glue	______
3 ______		______
4 ______		______

Directions Provide small objects like those pictured. Have children estimate the weight of each object in cubes, weigh the object, and record the number.

Name ______________________________

Temperature

P 6-11

1. 

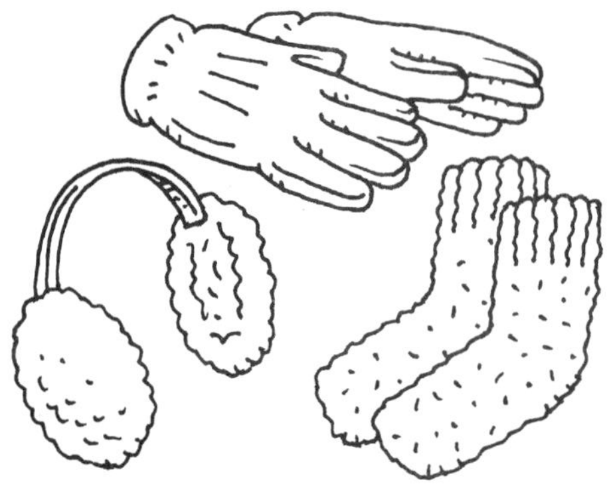
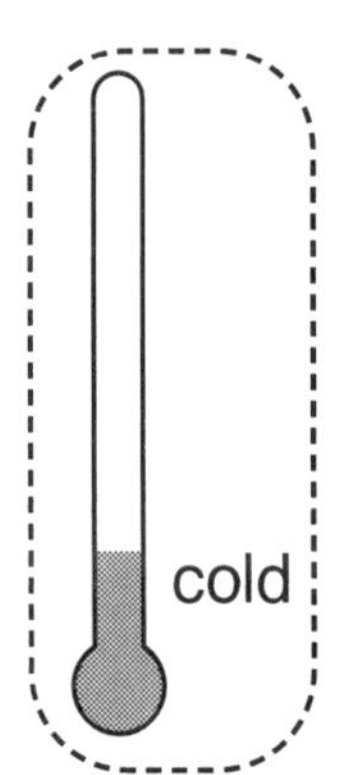

2. 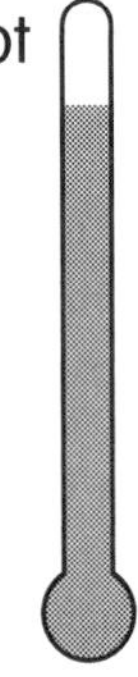

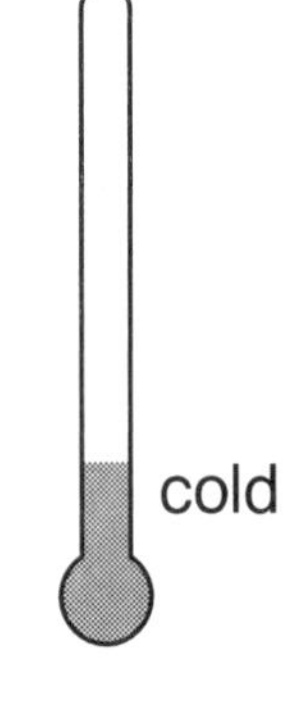

3. 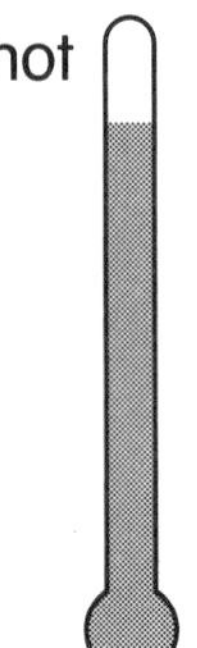

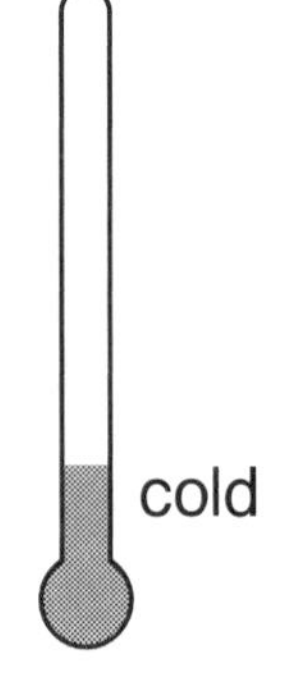

4. 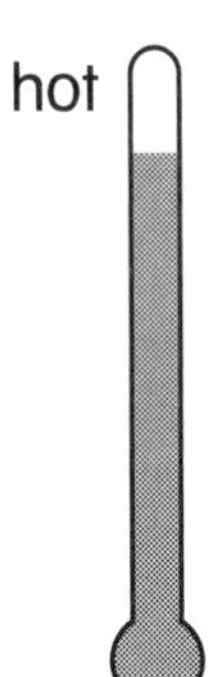

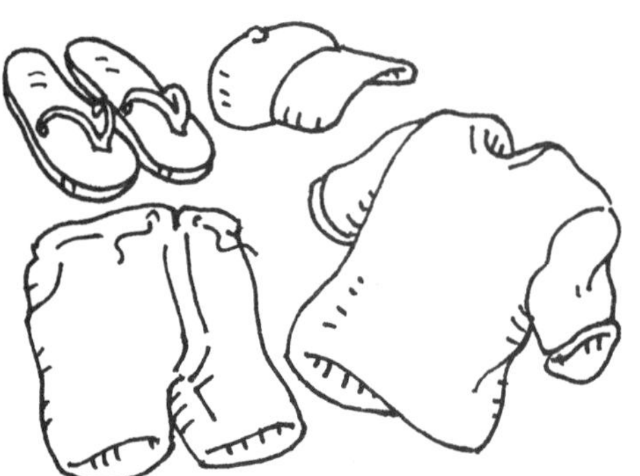
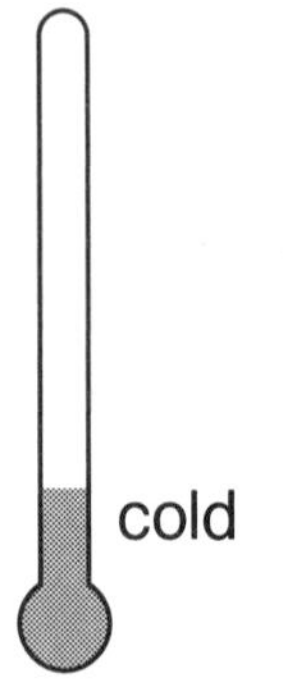

Directions In each exercise have children circle the thermometer showing the temperature when they might wear the items of clothing.

Name ____________________

PROBLEM-SOLVING APPLICATIONS **P 6-12**

Around the Home

1

2

Directions In Exercise 1 have children mark an *X* on the containers that will hold less than the watering can. In Exercise 2 have children circle the objects that are heavier than the flashlight.

Name ____________________

Days of the Week

P 7-1

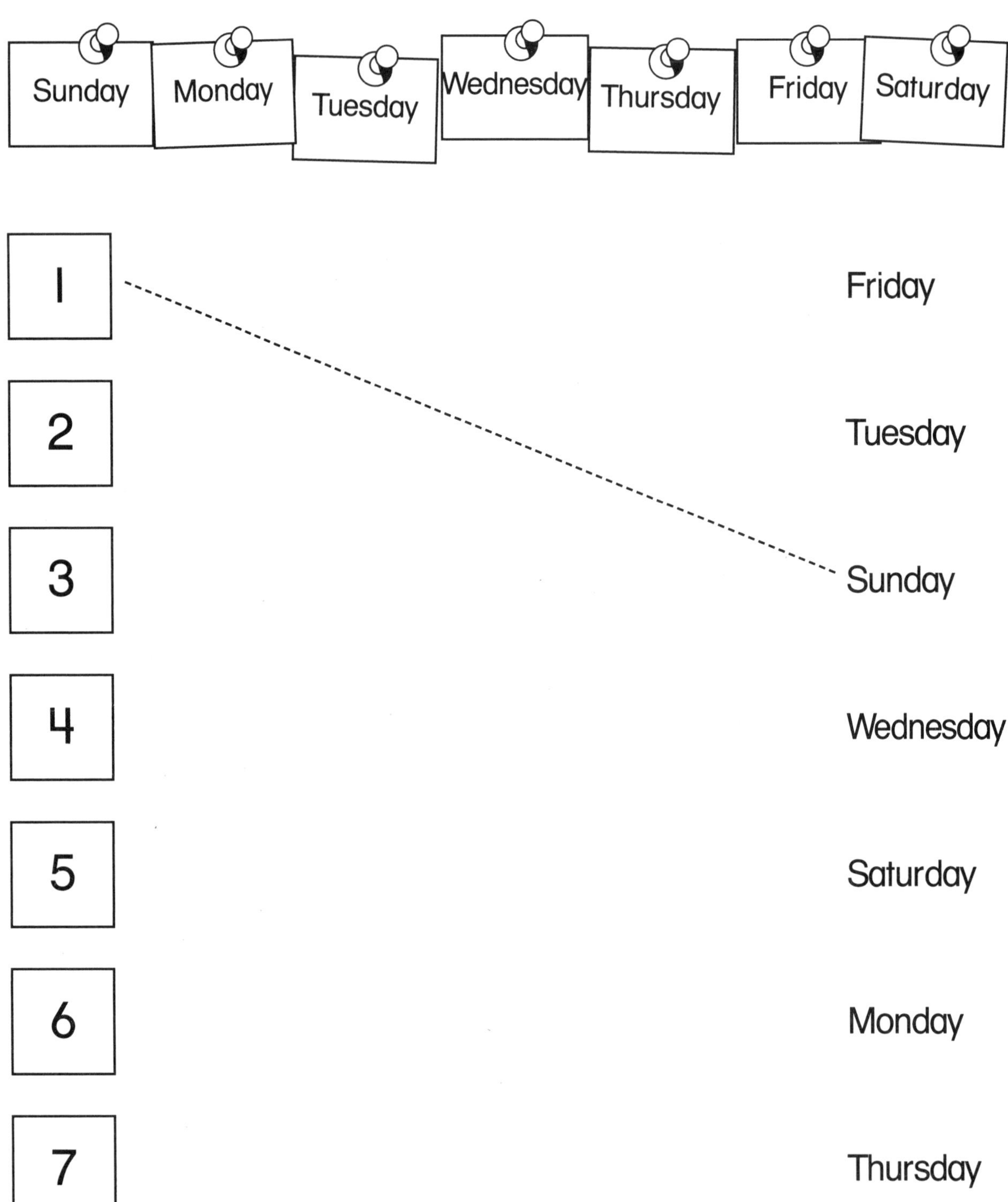

Directions Have children put the days of the week in order by drawing a line to match each day with a number.

Name ______________________________

Yesterday, Today, and Tomorrow

P 7-2

Sunday	Monday	Tuesday	Wednesday	Thursday	Friday	Saturday

If today is

______________________________.

Yesterday was

______________________________.

Tomorrow will be

______________________________.

Directions Have children circle the day of the week that the teacher identifies as today, mark an *X* on the day that was yesterday, and underline the day that will be tomorrow. Then have children complete the sentences.

Name ______

Months and Seasons

P 7-3

Directions In Exercise 1, have children circle the current month and mark an *X* on the last month of the year. In Exercise 2, have children mark an *X* on the current season.

Name ____________________

Calendar

P 7-4

April

Sunday	Monday	Tuesday	Wednesday	Thursday	Friday	Saturday
	1	2		4	5	6
7		9	10	11		13
14	15		17		19	20
21		23		25	26	
28	29	30				

Directions Have children trace the name of the month and the dates on the calendar. Then have children fill in the missing dates and circle the days of the week.

Name ____________________

Ordering Events

Directions In Exercise 1, have children draw a line to the picture that shows what happens next. In Exercises 2 and 3, have children order the events from first to last using the numbers 1, 2, and 3.

Name ______________________________

Time of Day

P 7-6

Directions In each exercise have children match the picture with the symbol for morning, afternoon, and evening.

Name ___________________________________

Telling Time on an Analog Clock

P 7-7

3 o'clock

6 o'clock

10 o'clock

8 o'clock

4 o'clock

5 o'clock

Directions In each exercise have children draw the hour hand to show the time.

Name ______________________________

Telling Time on a Digital Clock

P 7-8

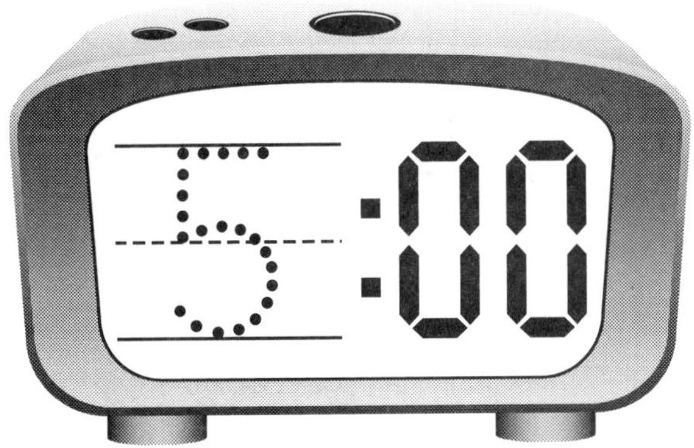

5 o'clock

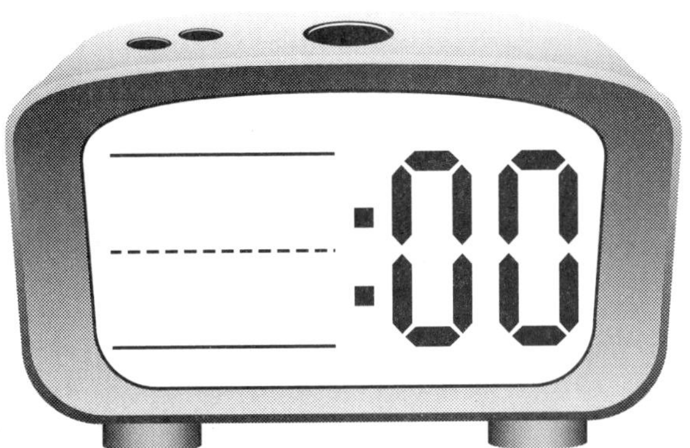

11 o'clock

_______ o'clock

Directions In Exercises 1 and 2, have children show the time by recording a number on the digital clock and drawing the hour hand on the analog clock. In Exercise 3, have children choose a time, record it on the write-on line, and show the time on the digital and analog clocks.

Name ____________________

More Time and Less Time

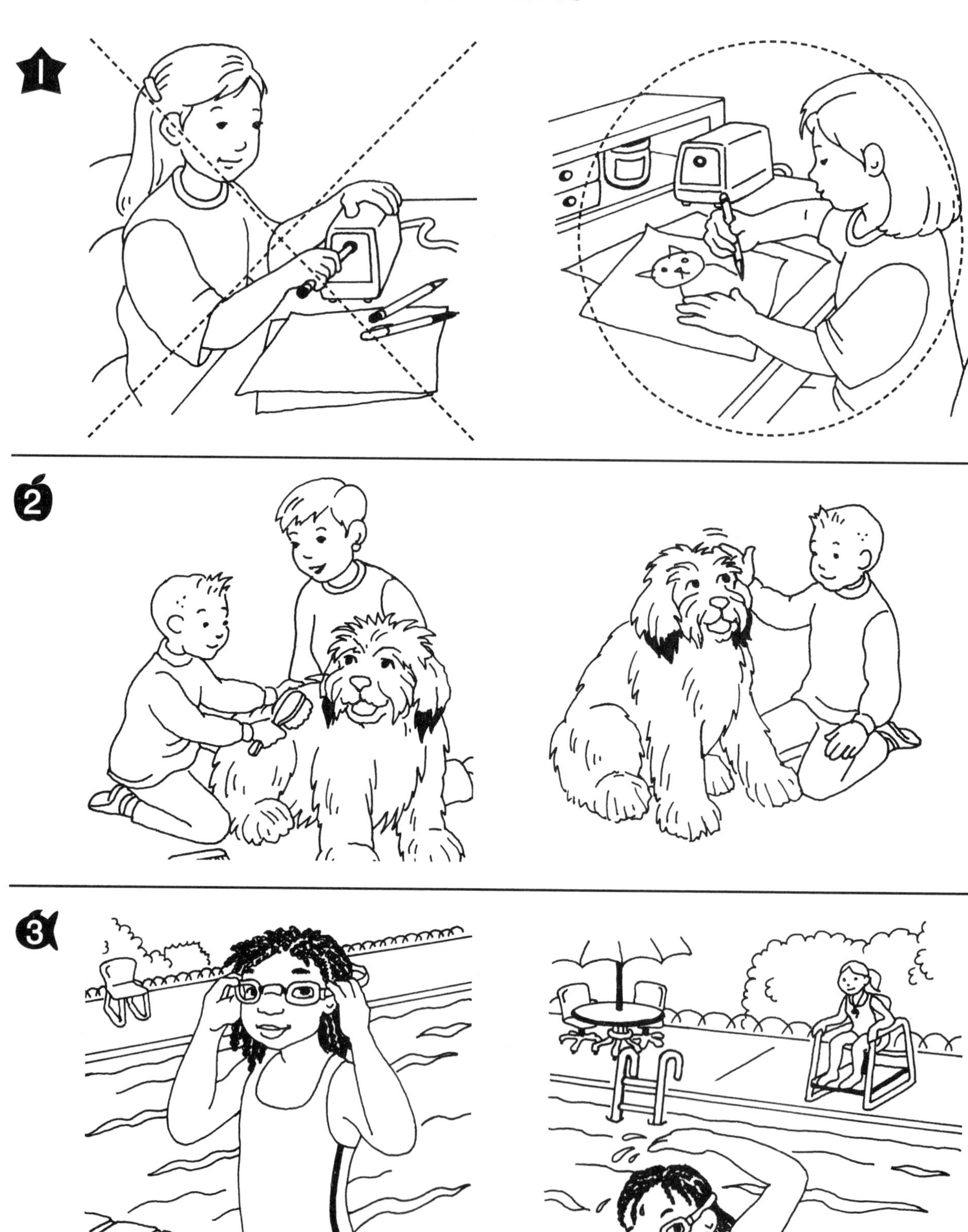

Directions In each exercise have children place an *X* on the event that takes less time and circle the event that takes more time.

Name ______________________________

Penny

5¢ 4¢ 6¢

7¢ 9¢ 10¢

3

2¢ 6¢ 5¢

4

8¢ 10¢ 7¢

Directions In each exercise have children count the pennies and circle the correct value.

Name ____________________

Nickel

P 7-11

9¢ 10¢ 6¢

8¢ 7¢ 10¢

7¢ 5¢ 3¢

10¢ 6¢ 8¢

Directions Have children figure out the value of each group of coins and circle the correct number.

Name ______________________________

Dime

P 7-12

2¢  5¢

2

1¢ 5¢ 10¢

3

5¢ 10¢ 7¢

4

10¢ 9¢ 8¢

Directions Have children figure out the value of each group of coins and circle the correct number.

Name ______________________________

PROBLEM-SOLVING STRATEGY **P 7-13**

Act It Out

1

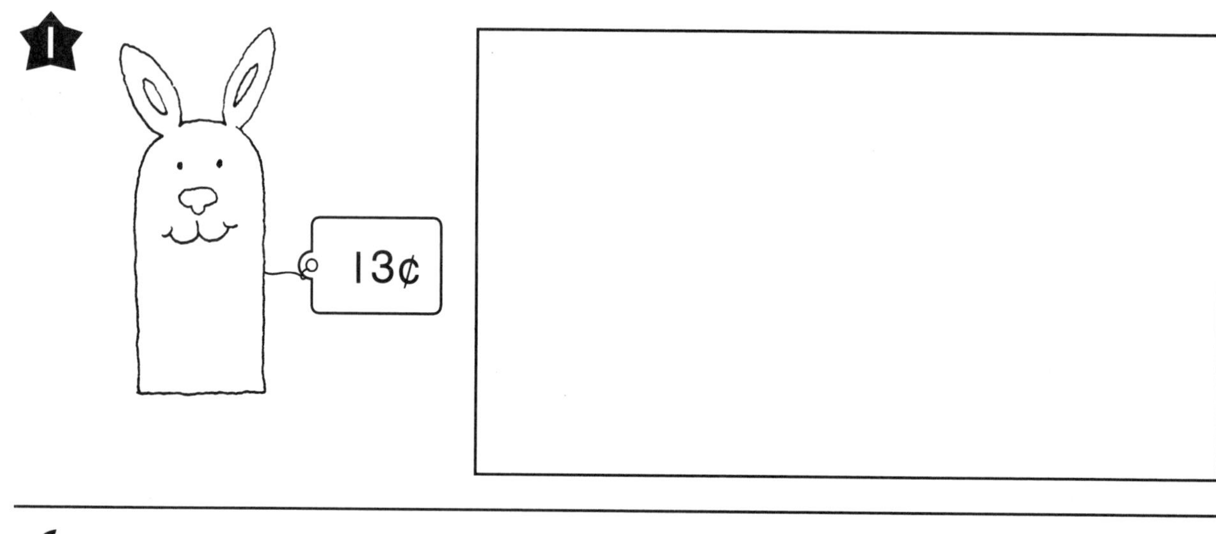

2

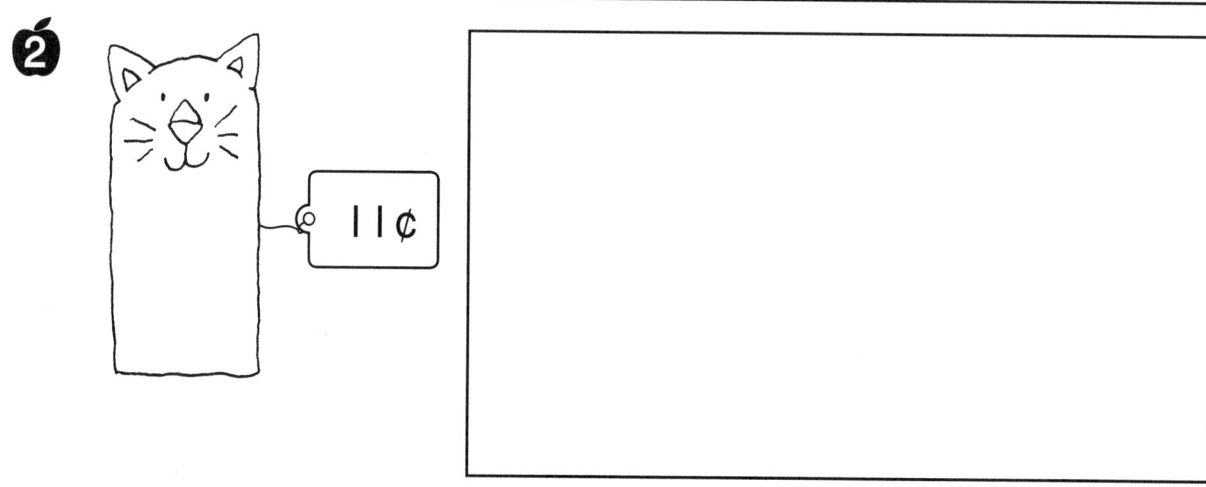

3

Directions Give children coins. Have them show the value of each item in different ways and then draw pictures of coins to show the value in one way.

Name ____________________

Quarter and Dollar

Directions Have children identify the coins or bills on the left and circle the coin or bill on the right that belongs in the group.

Name ______________________

Comparing Values

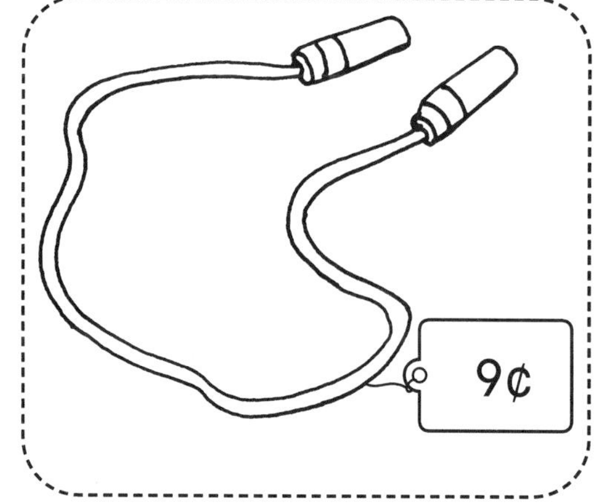

2

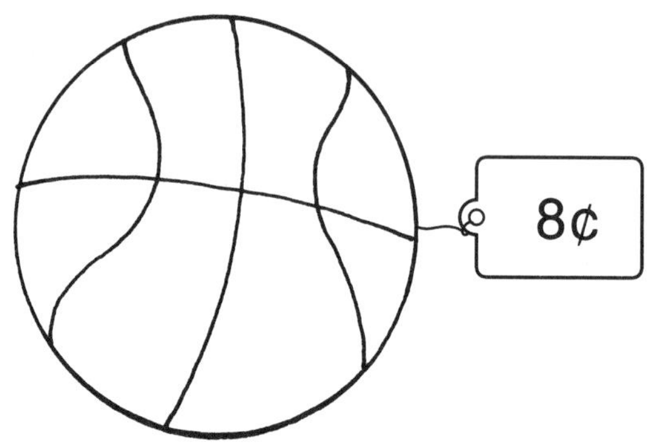

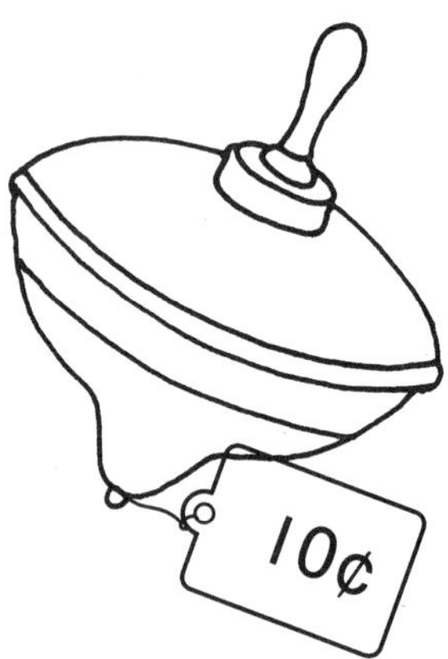

3

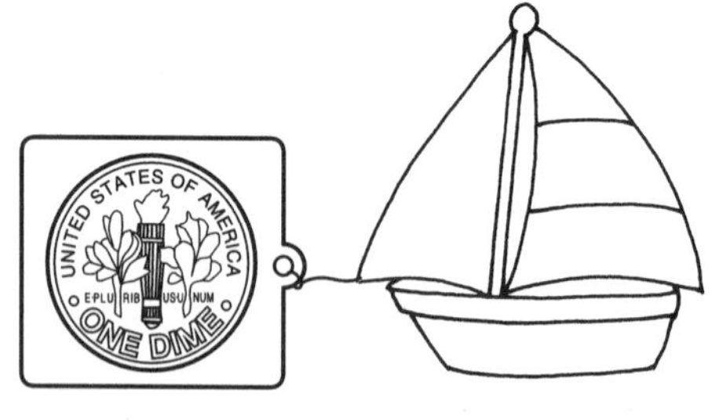

Directions In Exercises 1 and 2, have children circle the item that costs more. In Exercise 3, have children mark an *X* on the item that costs less.

Name ______________________________

PROBLEM-SOLVING APPLICATIONS **P 7-16**

Time to Play

2

5¢

4¢

25¢

1¢

7¢

10¢

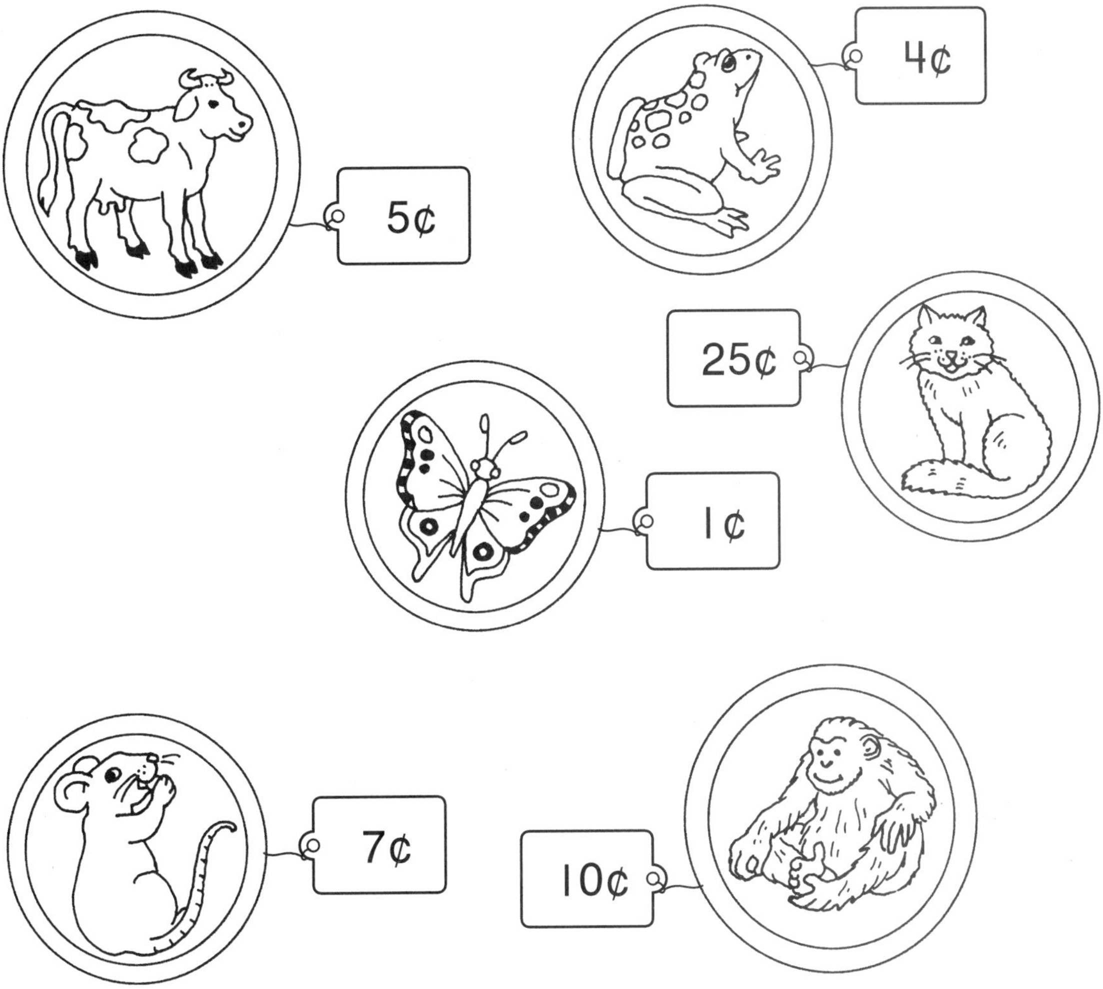

Directions In Exercise 1, tell children that some friends had a play date at 3 o'clock. Ask children to circle the clock that shows the time. In Exercise 2, have children circle the stickers they can buy using only one coin.

Name ___________________________

Solid Figures

P 8-1

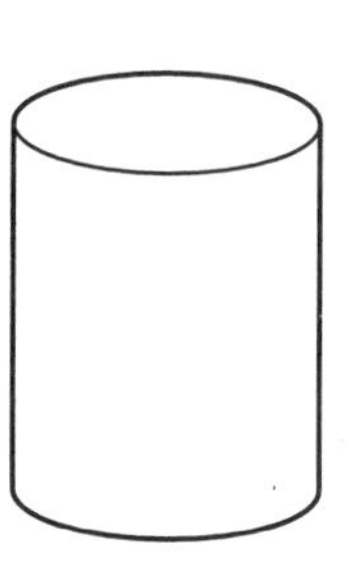

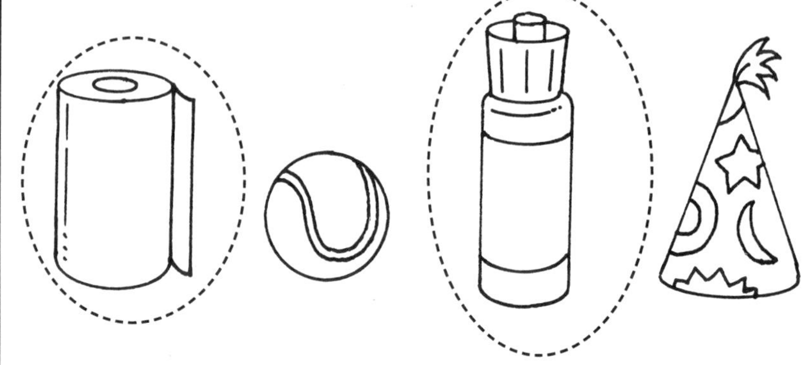

2

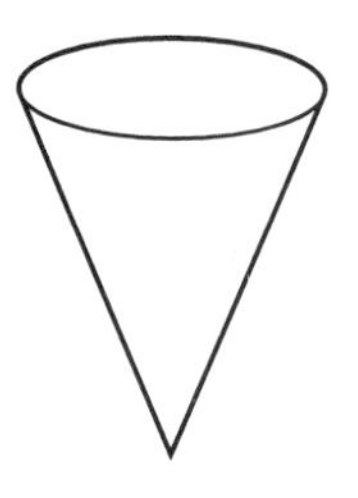

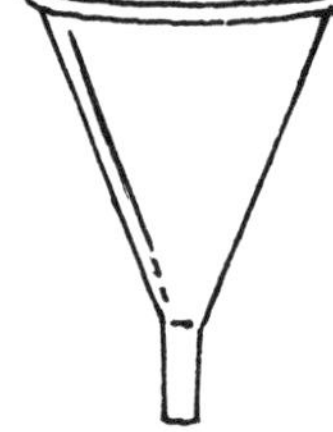

3

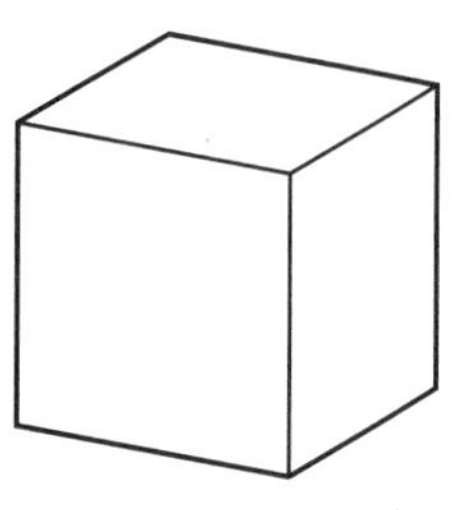

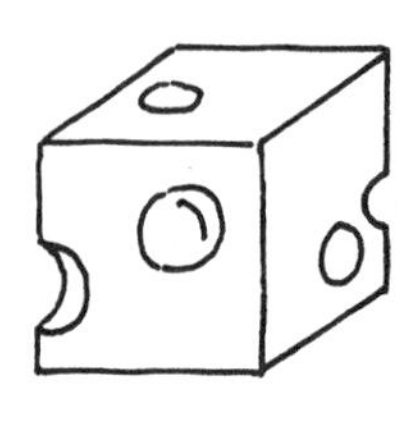

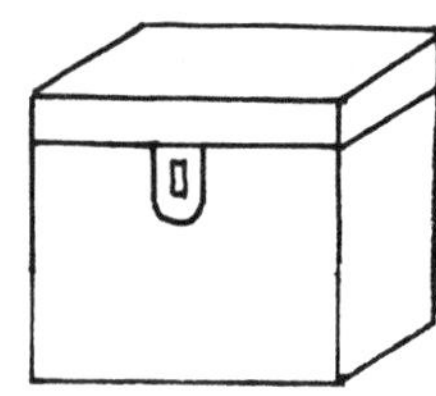

4

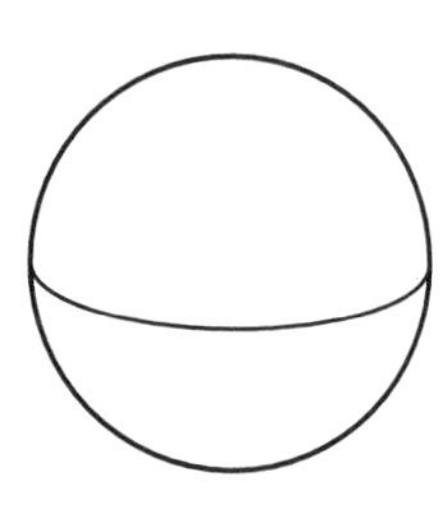

Directions In each exercise have children circle the everyday objects that have the same shape as the solid figure.

Name ___________________________________

Comparing Solid Figures

P 8-2

Directions Have children circle each item that can roll. Then have them mark an *X* on each item that can slide. Point out that some items that are circled should also be marked with an *X*.

Name ______________________________

Flat Surfaces on Solid Figures

P 8-3

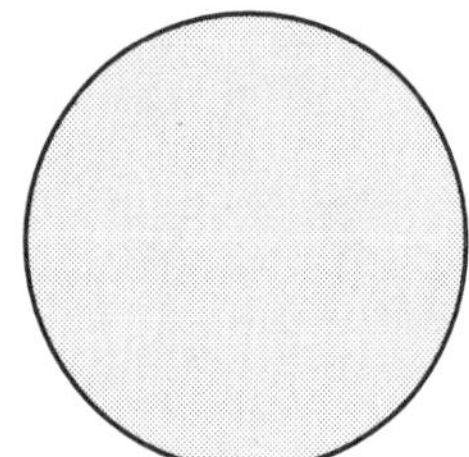

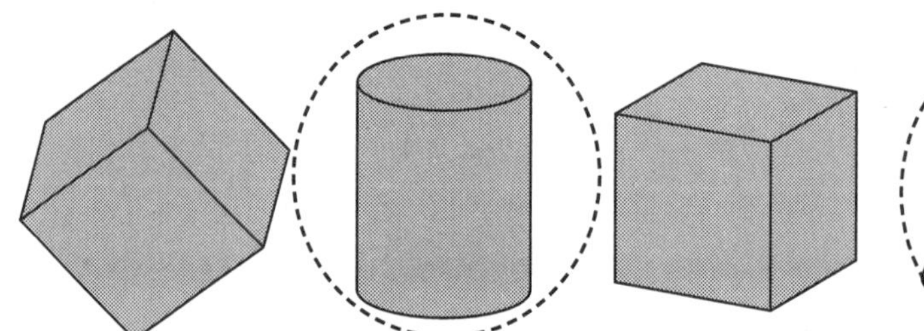

2

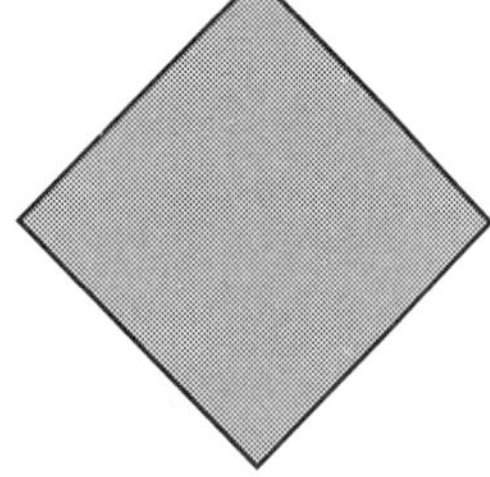

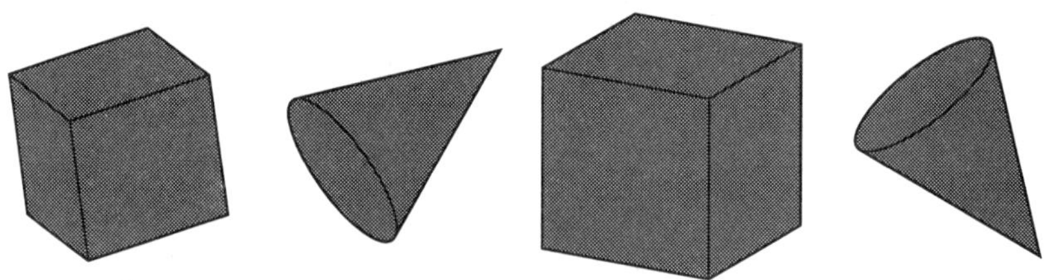

3

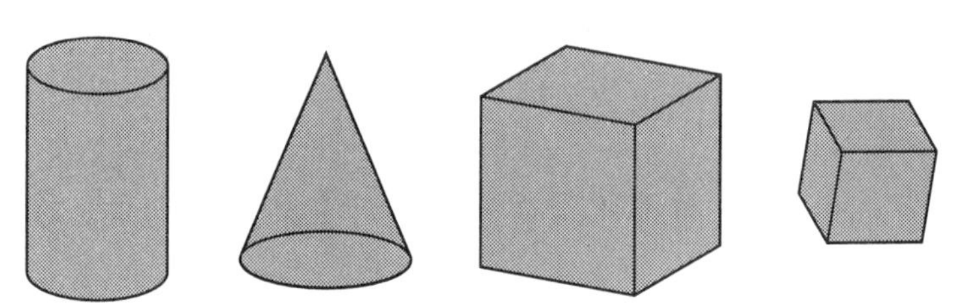

4

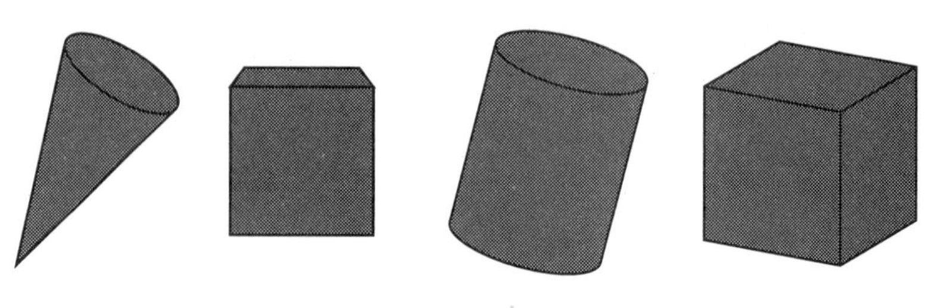

Directions In each exercise have children circle the solid figures with a flat surface that matches the shape on the left.

Name ______________________________

Squares and Other Rectangles

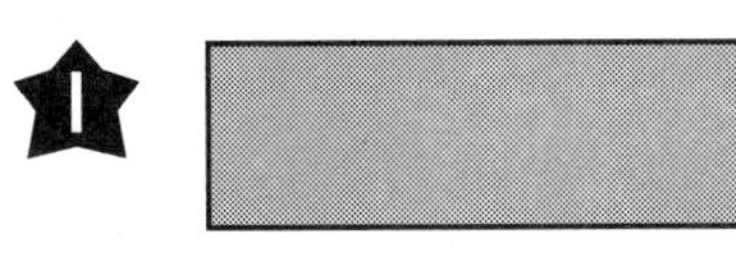

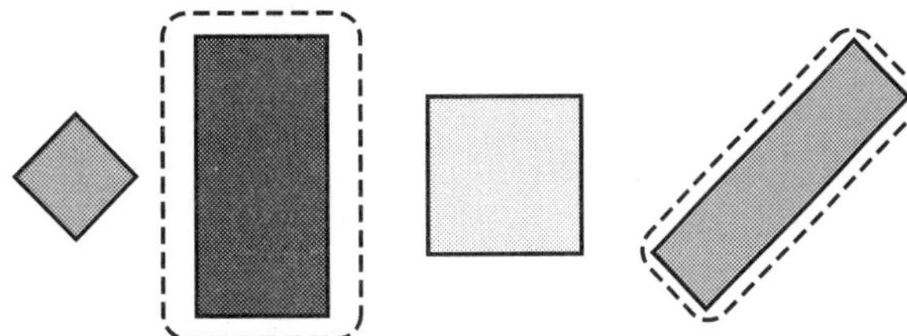

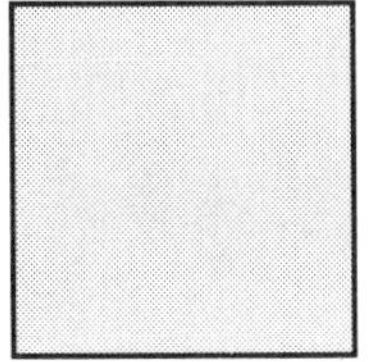

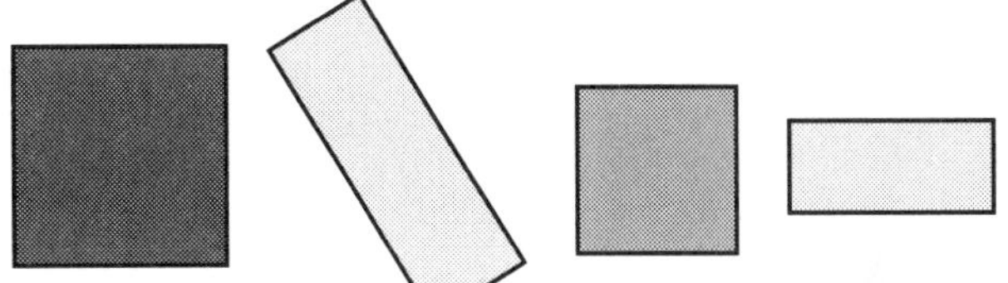

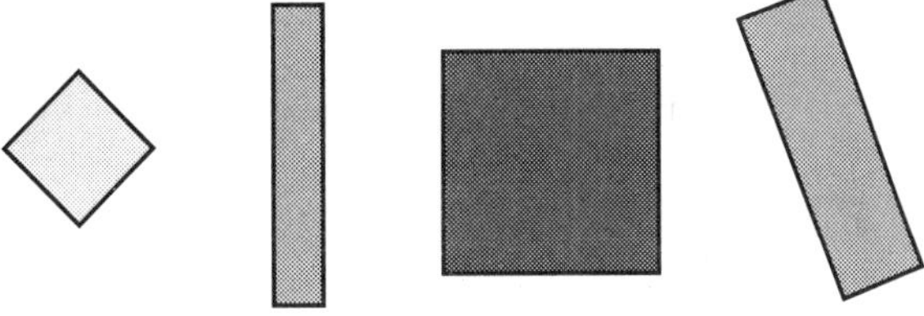

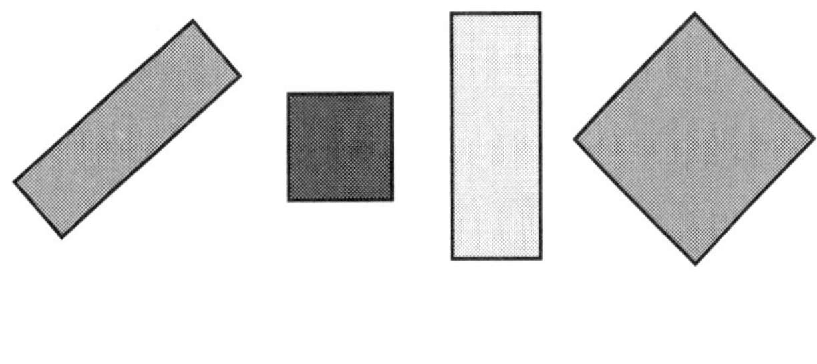

Directions In each exercise have children circle the shapes on the right that are the same as the shapes on the left.

Name ___________________________________

Circles and Triangles

P 8-5

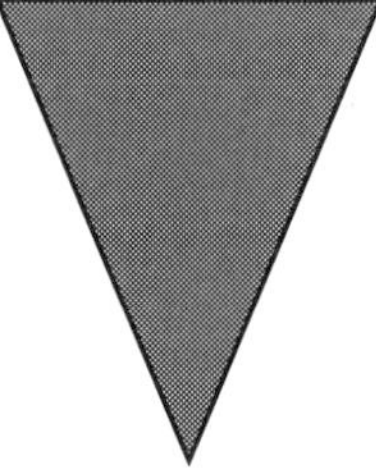

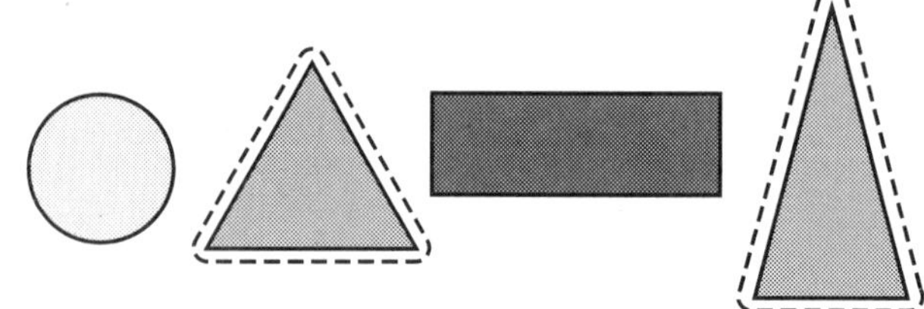

2

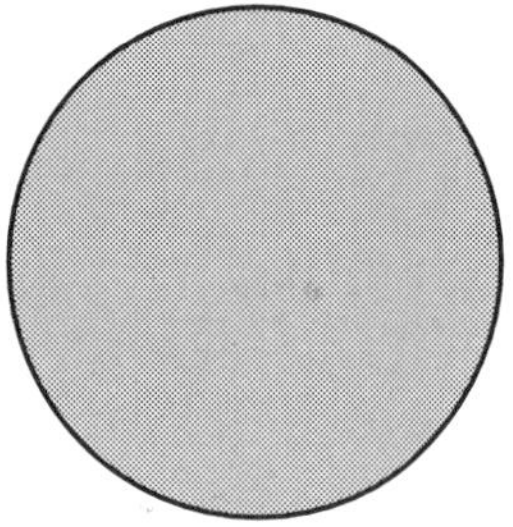

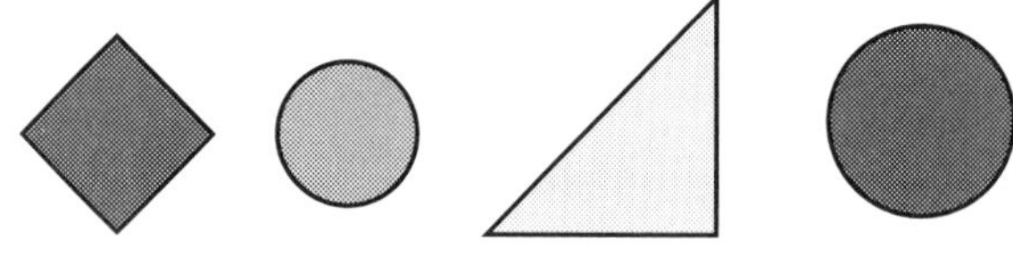

3

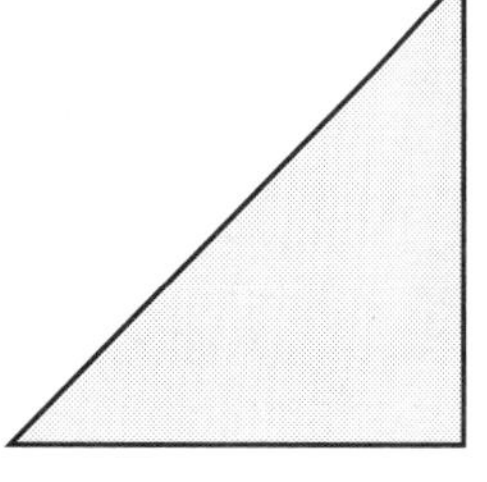

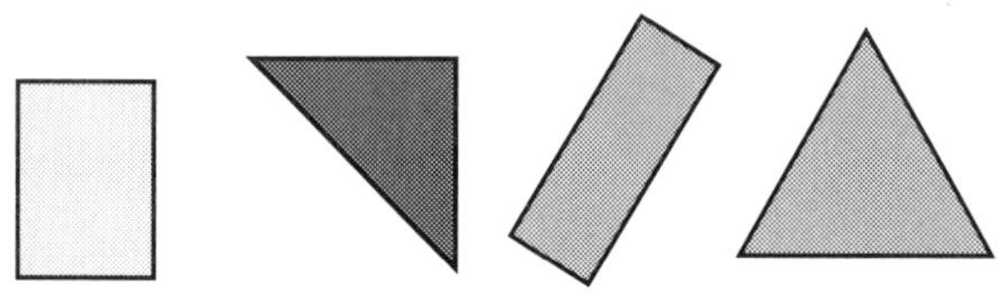

4

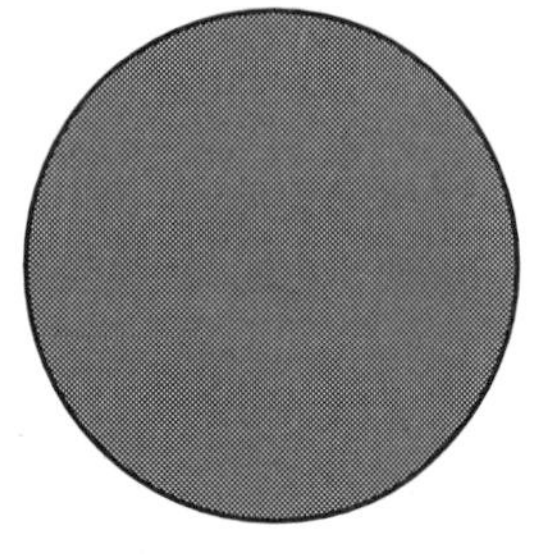

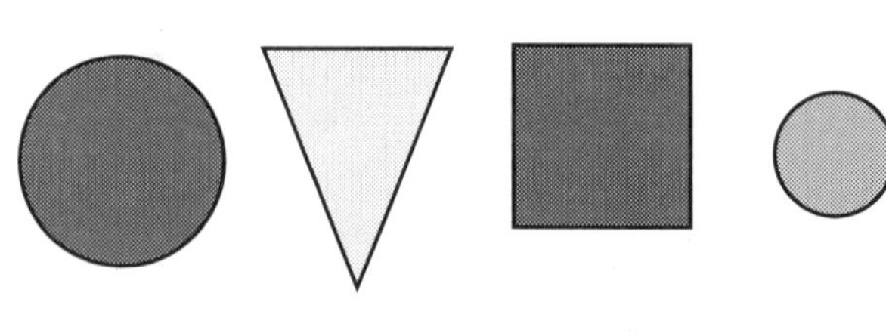

Directions In each exercise have children circle the shapes that are the same as the shape on the left.

Name ______________________________

Slides, Flips, and Turns

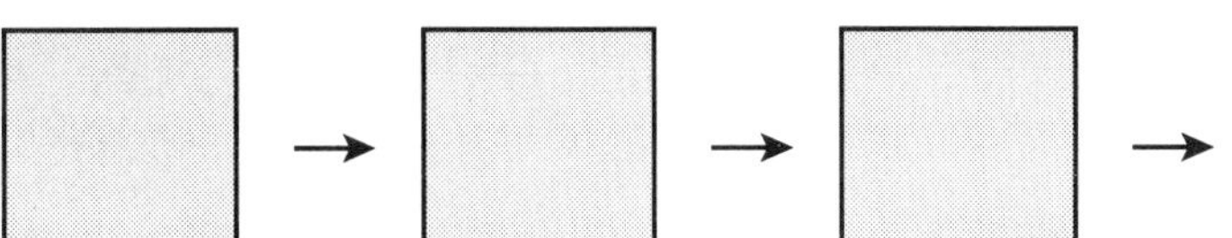

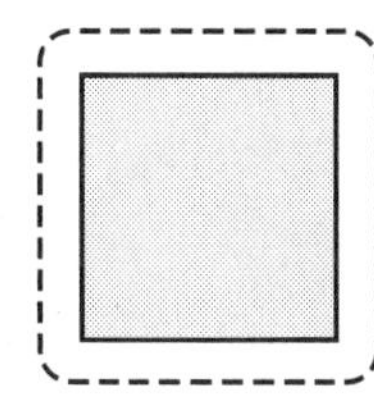

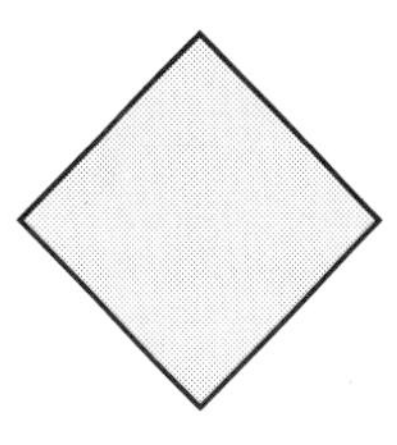

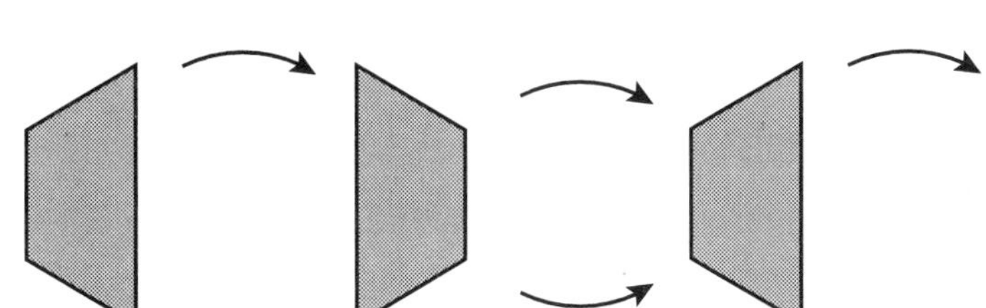

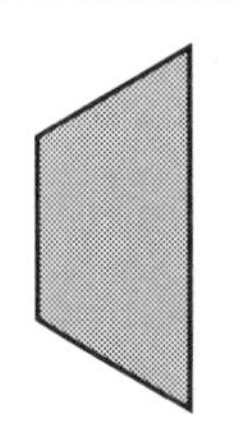

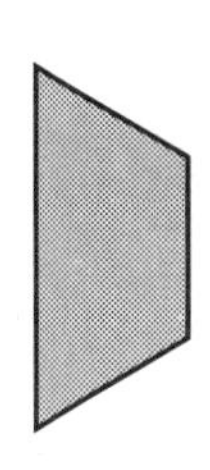

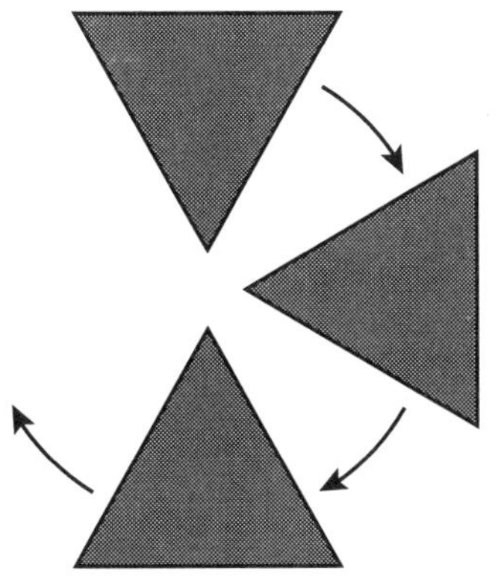

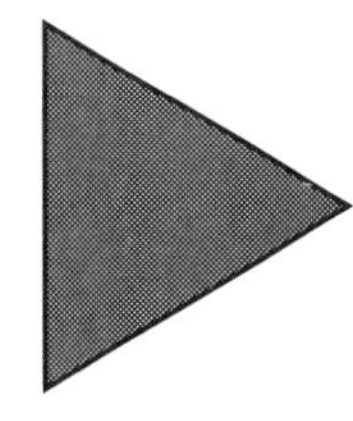

Directions In Exercise 1 have children circle the block that comes next when you slide it. In Exercise 2 have children circle the block that comes next when you flip it. In Exercise 3 have children circle the block that comes next when you turn it.

Name ______________________________

Combining and Separating Shapes

P 8-7

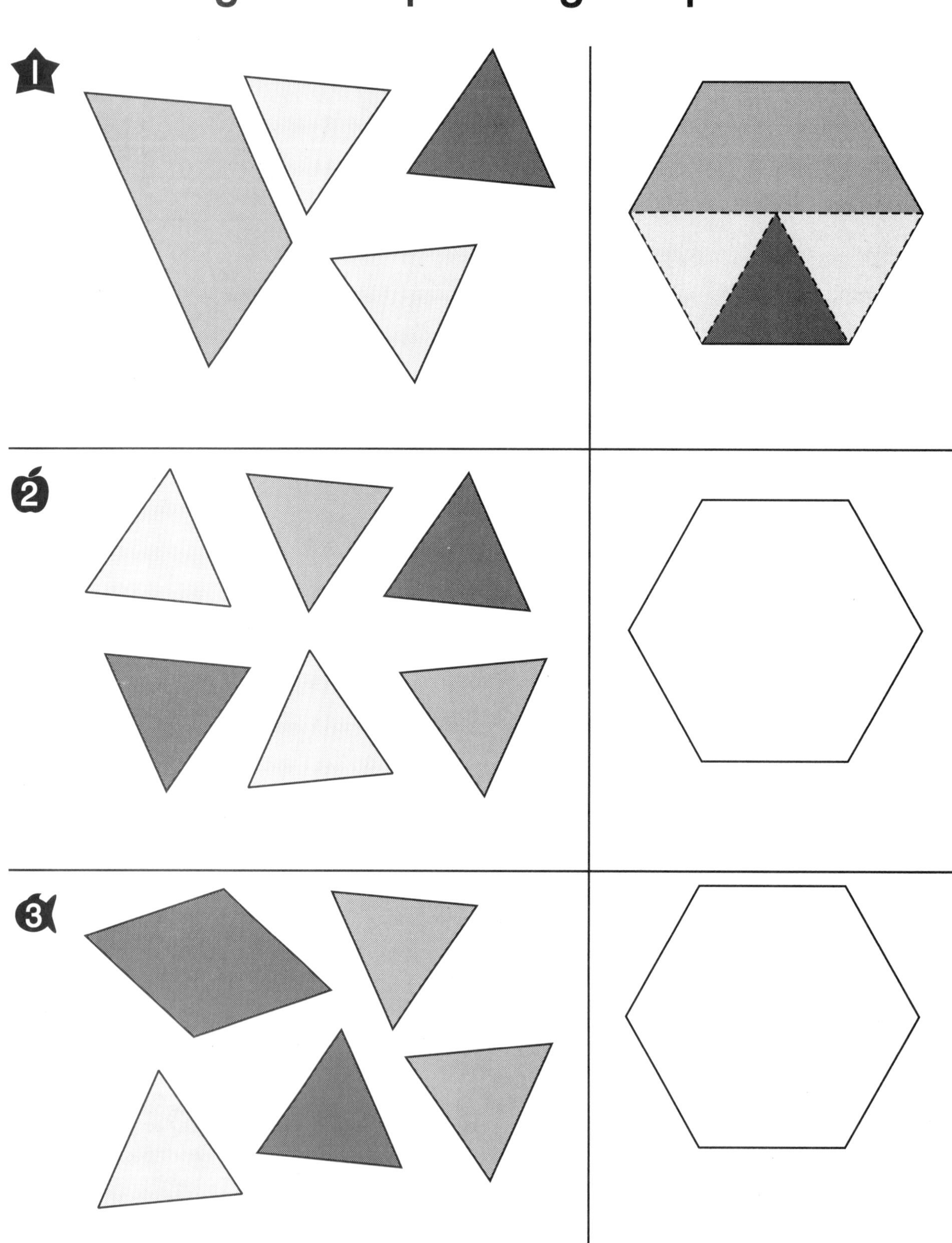

Directions Have children use the pattern blocks on the left to cover the larger shape on the right. Have them draw and color the pattern blocks to show how they covered the larger shape.

Name ____________________

Symmetry

P 8-8

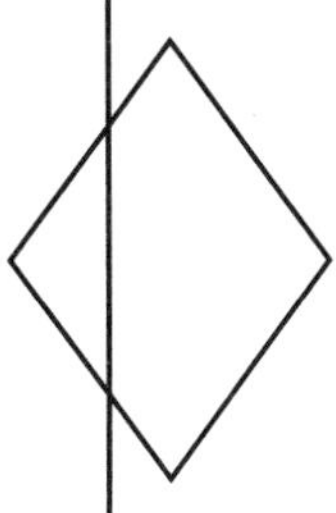
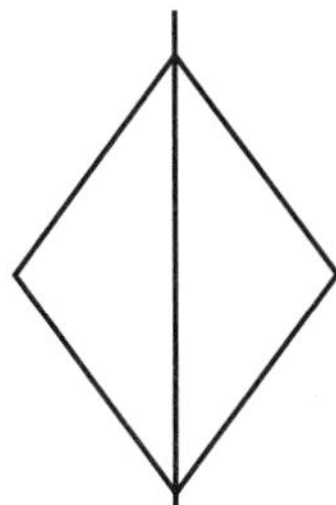
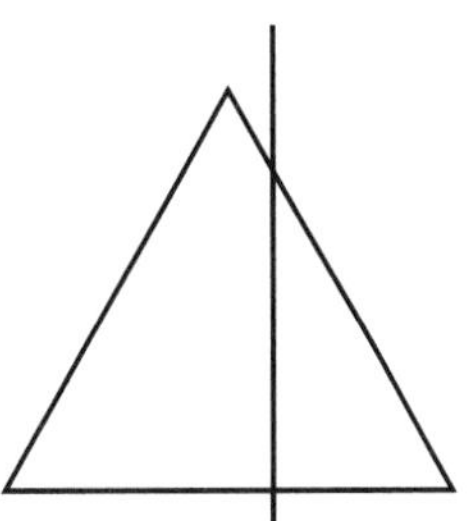
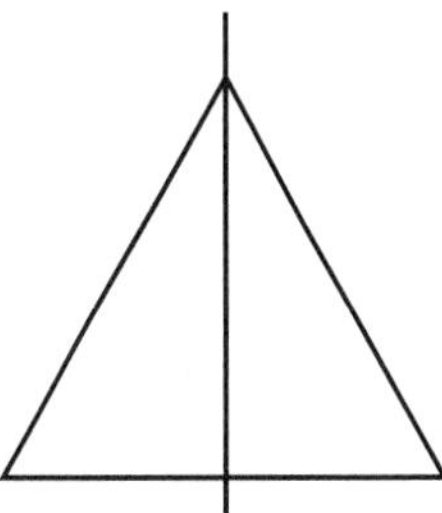

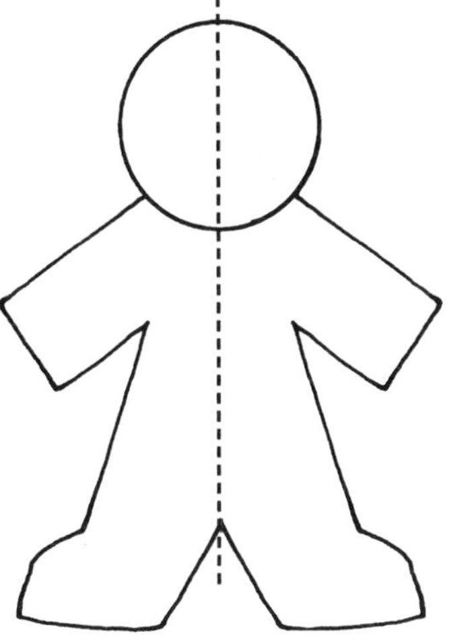
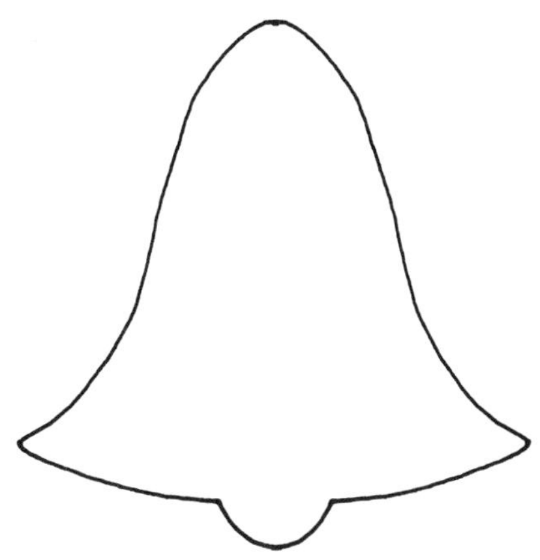

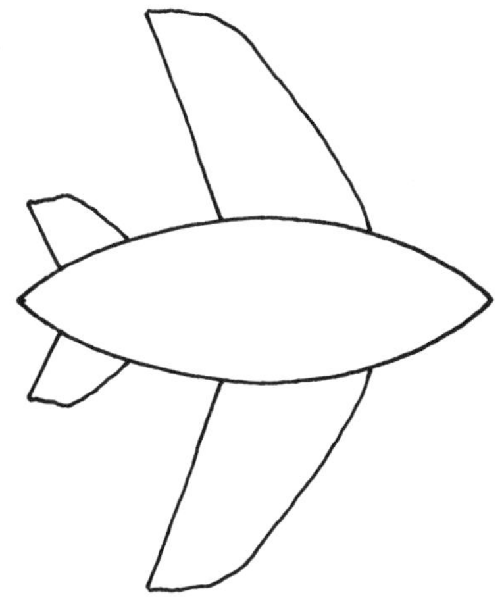

Directions In Exercise 1 have children circle the shapes that show matching parts. In Exercises 2 and 3 have children draw a line through each item to show matching parts.

Name ______________________________

Equal Parts

P 8-9

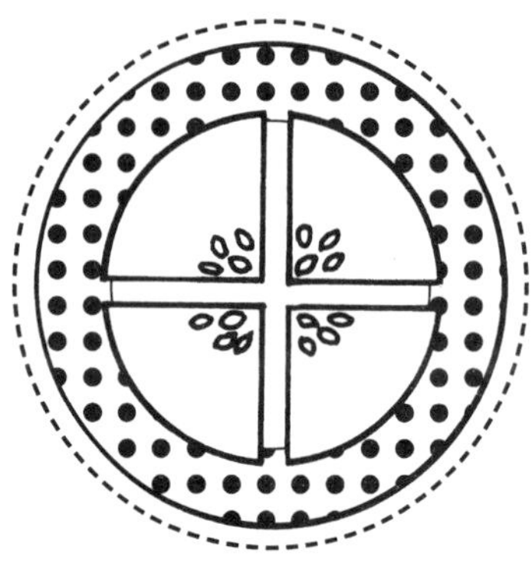

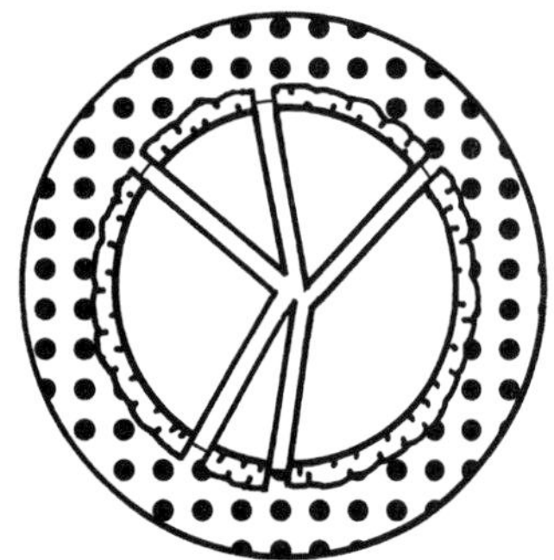

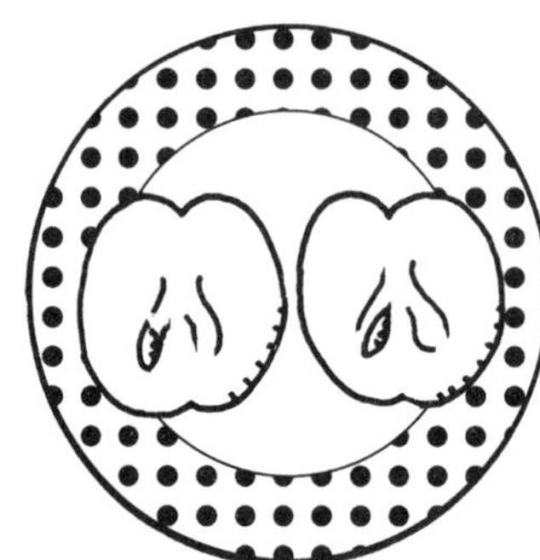

Directions Have children circle the items that are cut into equal parts.

Name ____________________

Halves and Fourths

P 8-10

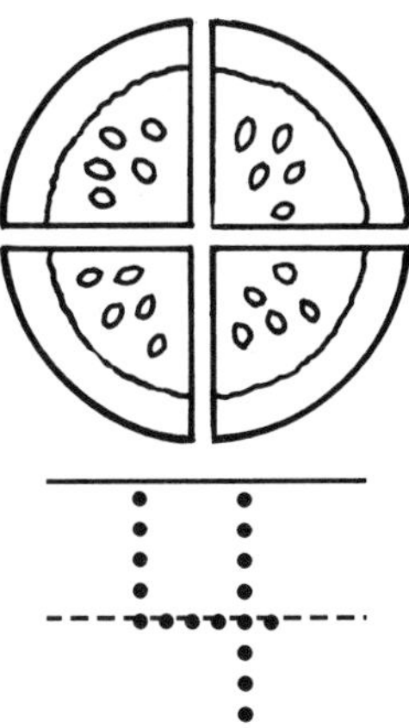

2

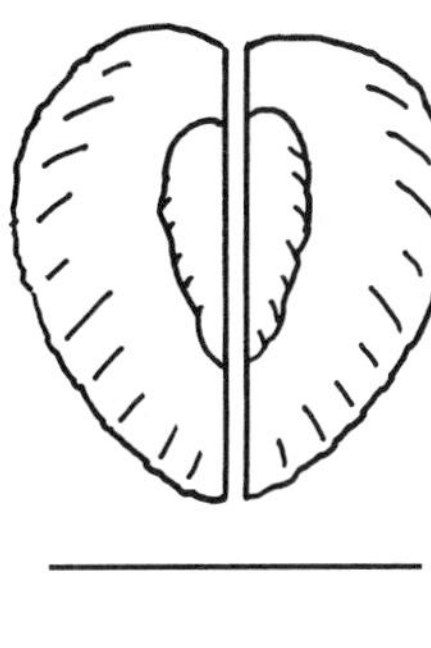

3

4

5

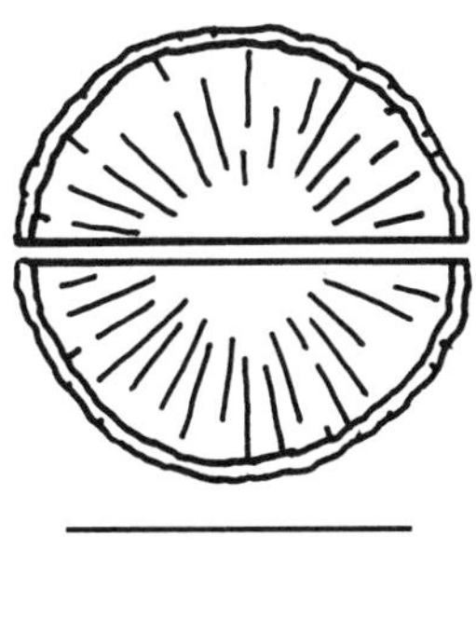

6

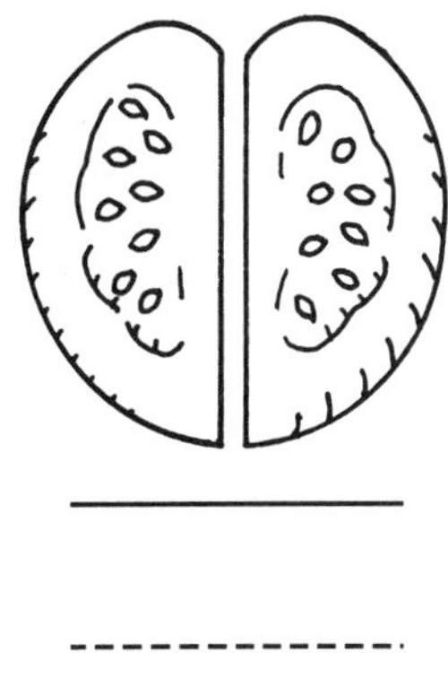

Directions In each exercise have children write the number that tells how many equal shares each item shows.

Name ____________________

PROBLEM-SOLVING STRATEGY **P 8-11**

Use Objects

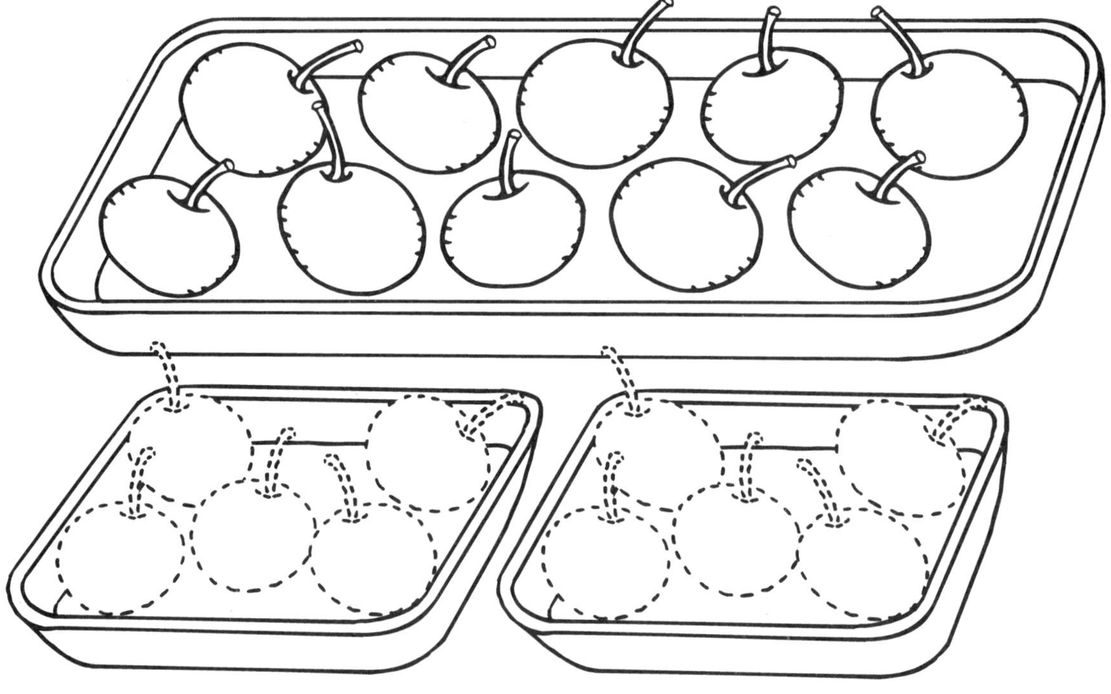

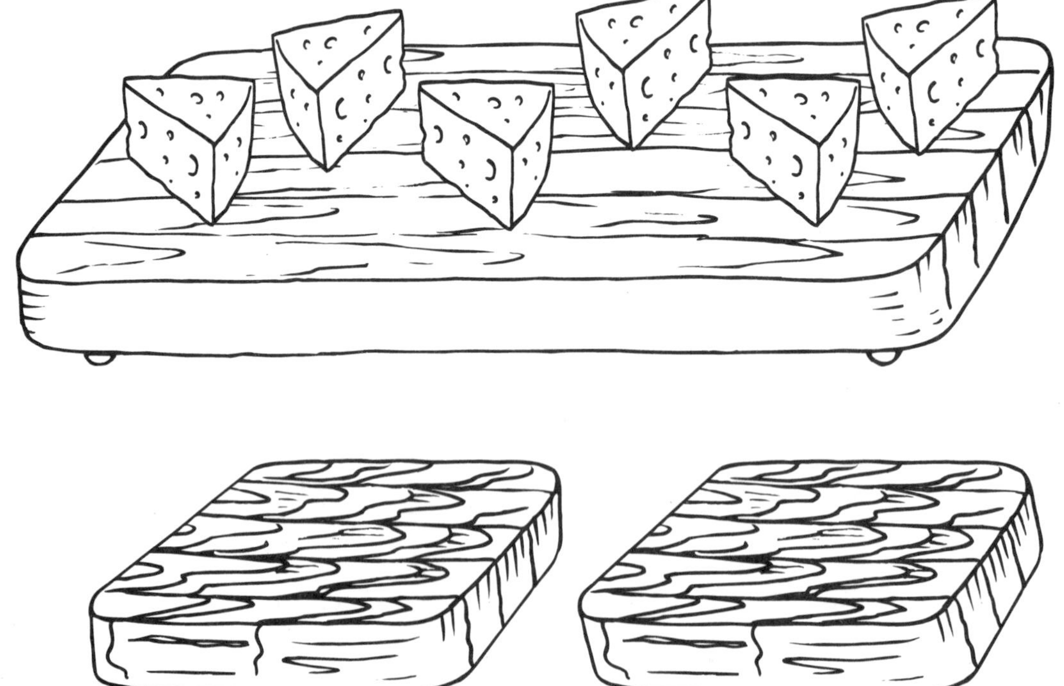

Directions Have children place counters on each item and then make equal shares on the plates. Have them show the equal shares by drawing cherries in Exercise 1 and drawing cheese wedges in Exercise 2.

Name ___

PROBLEM-SOLVING APPLICATIONS **P 8-12**

I Spy

Sasha ___

Bob ___

2

Sasha ___

Bob ___

Directions Tell children that Sasha collects blocks and party hats. He wants to make equal shares of these things for himself and his friend Bob. Have children place counters on the objects in each group, figure out how many shares each child will have, and record the numbers.

Name ________________

Ways to Make 4 and 5

P 9-1

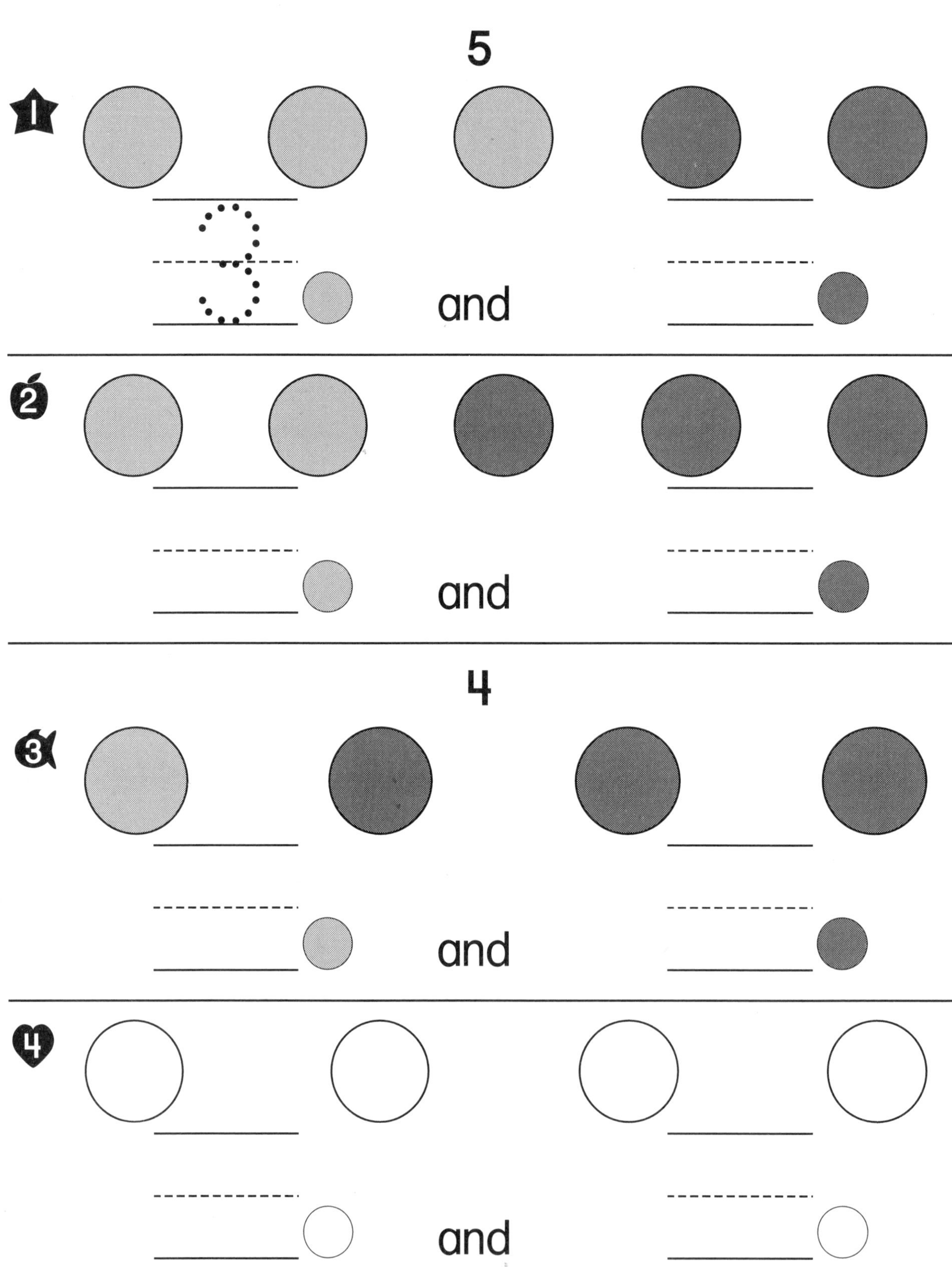

Directions Have children place matching counters in Exercises 1–3 and record the number of each color. In Exercise 4 have children use counters to show 4 in another way. Have them color the outlines to match the counters and record the number of each color.

Name ______________________________

Ways to Make 6 and 7

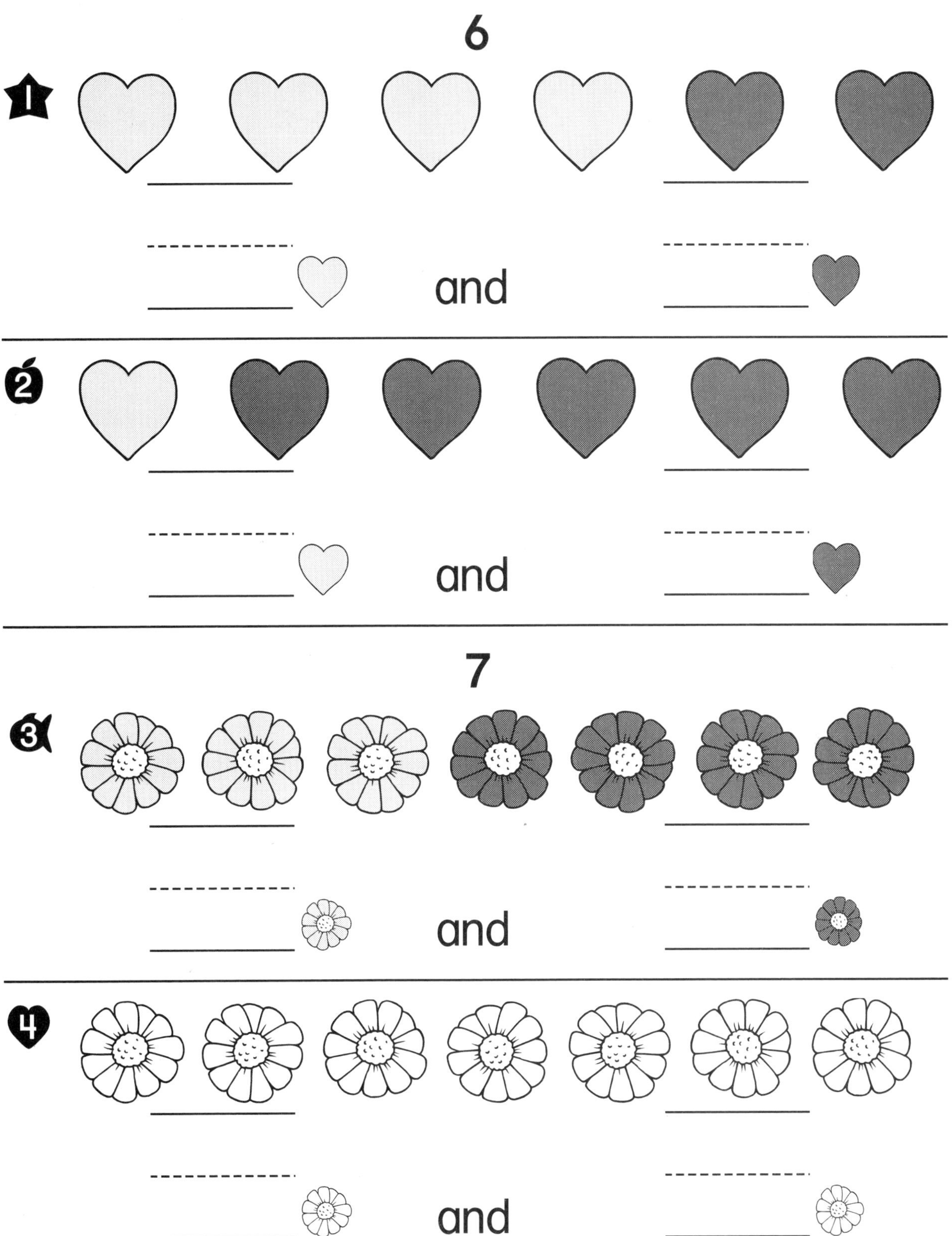

Directions In Exercises 1–3 have children count objects of each color and write the numbers. In Exercise 4 have children color to show a group of 7 daisies in two colors and write the numbers to show how many daisies of each color.

Name ____________________

Ways to Make 8 and 9

P 9-3

8

1

______ ______

______ and ______

2

______ ______

______ and ______

9

3

______ ______

______ and ______

4

______ ______

______ and ______

Directions In Exercises 1–3 have children count the insects of each color and write the numbers. In Exercise 4 have children color to show a group of 9 spiders in two colors and write the numbers to show how many spiders of each color.

Name ______________________________

Ways to Make 10

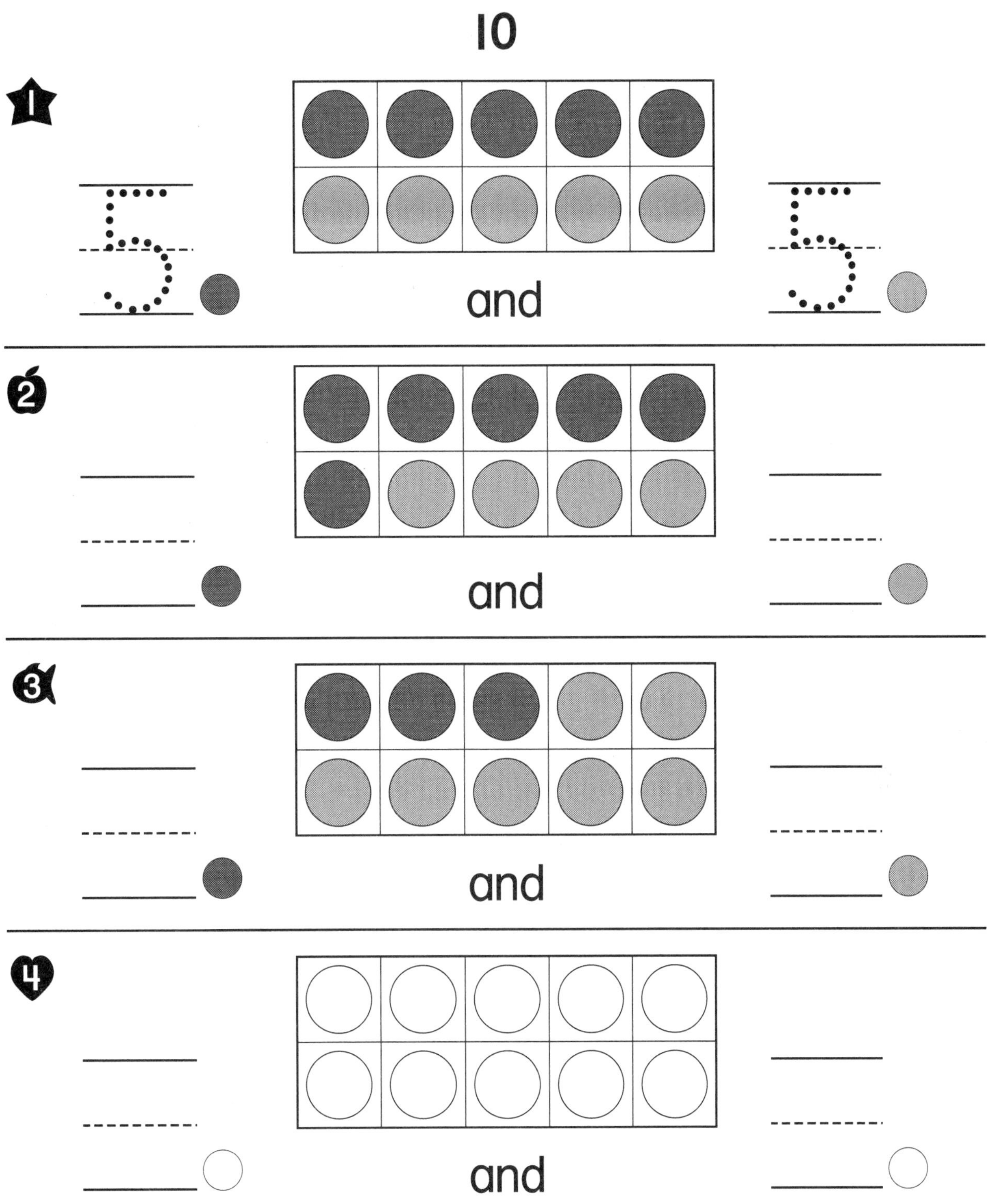

Directions In Exercises 1–3 have children count the counters and record the number of each color. In Exercise 4 have them show 10 in another way by coloring the counters red and yellow and recording the number of each color.

Name ____________________

PROBLEM-SOLVING STRATEGY **P 9-5**

Make an Organized List

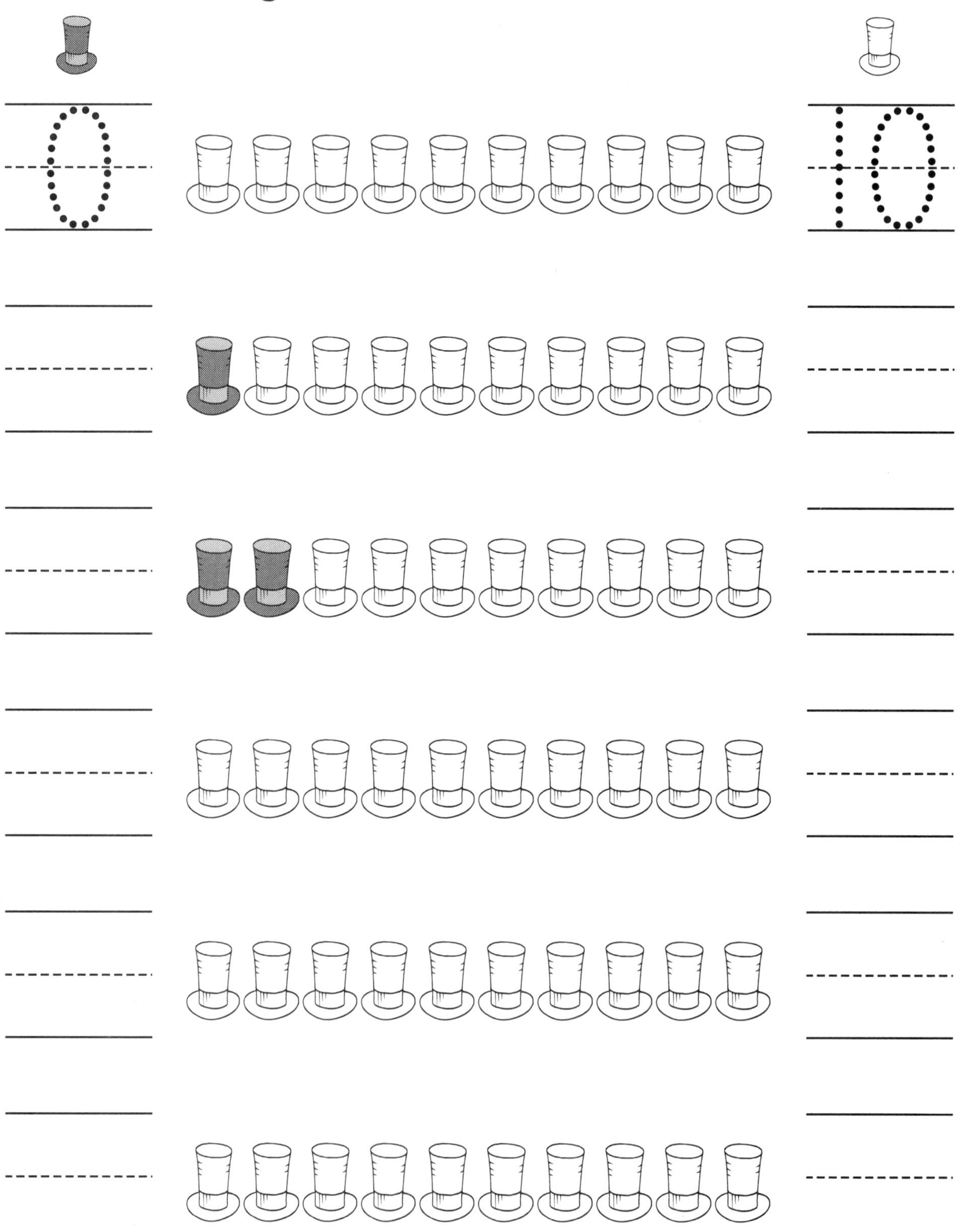

Directions Have children count each group of hats and record the number of hats in each group. Have them continue the pattern by coloring the hats two colors and writing the number of each color.

Name ____________________

I More and 2 More

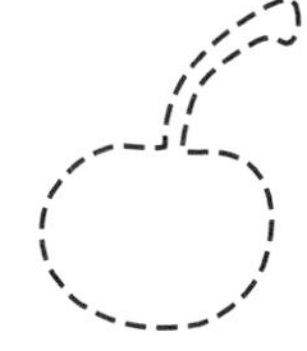

I and I more is 2.

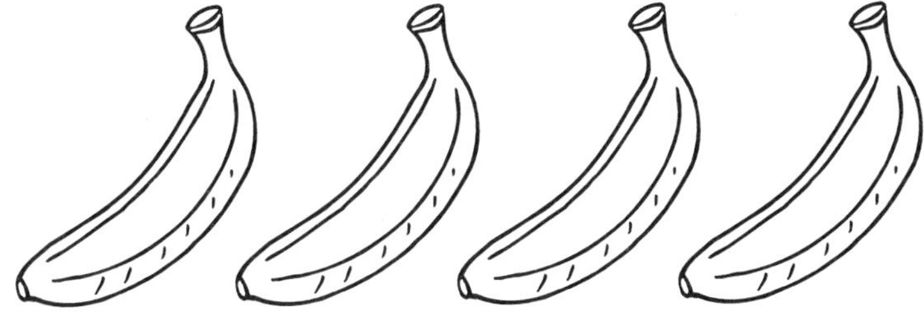

4 and I more is ______.

3 and 2 more is ______.

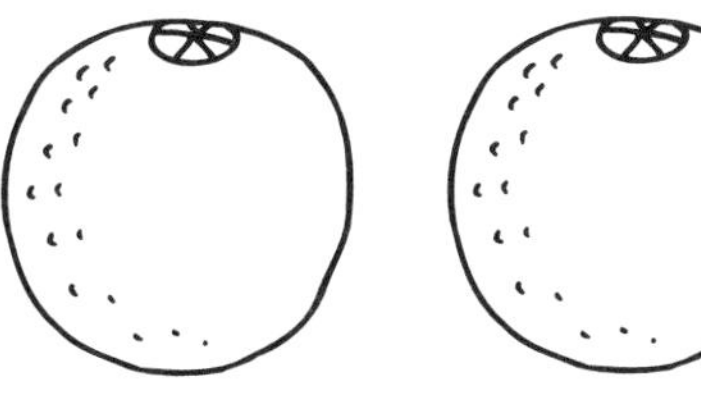

2 and 2 more is ______.

Directions In Exercises 1–2 have children draw 1 more object and record the number of objects in each group. In Exercises 3–4 repeat, drawing 2 more objects in each group.

Name ______________________________

I Fewer and 2 Fewer

P 9-7

I fewer than 5 is 4.

2

I fewer than 2 is ______.

3

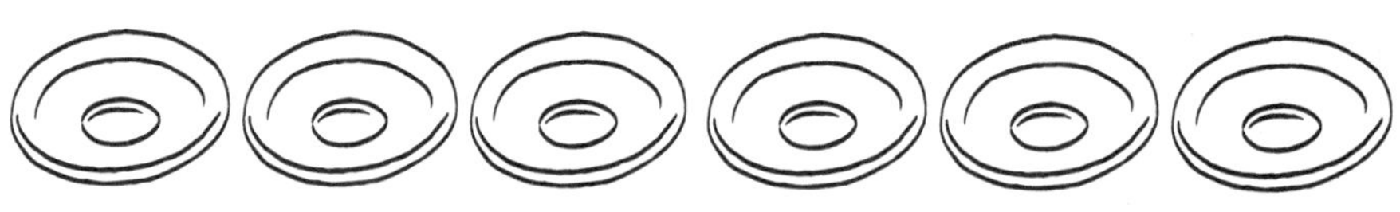

2 fewer than 6 is ______.

4

2 fewer than 4 is ______.

Directions In Exercises 1–2 have children mark an *X* on one of the objects in each group, count how many are left, and write the number. In Exercises 3–4 repeat, marking an *X* on two of the objects in each group.

Name ______________________________

PROBLEM-SOLVING APPLICATIONS **P 9-8**

Visit, Look, and Learn

1

8

________ and ________

2

5

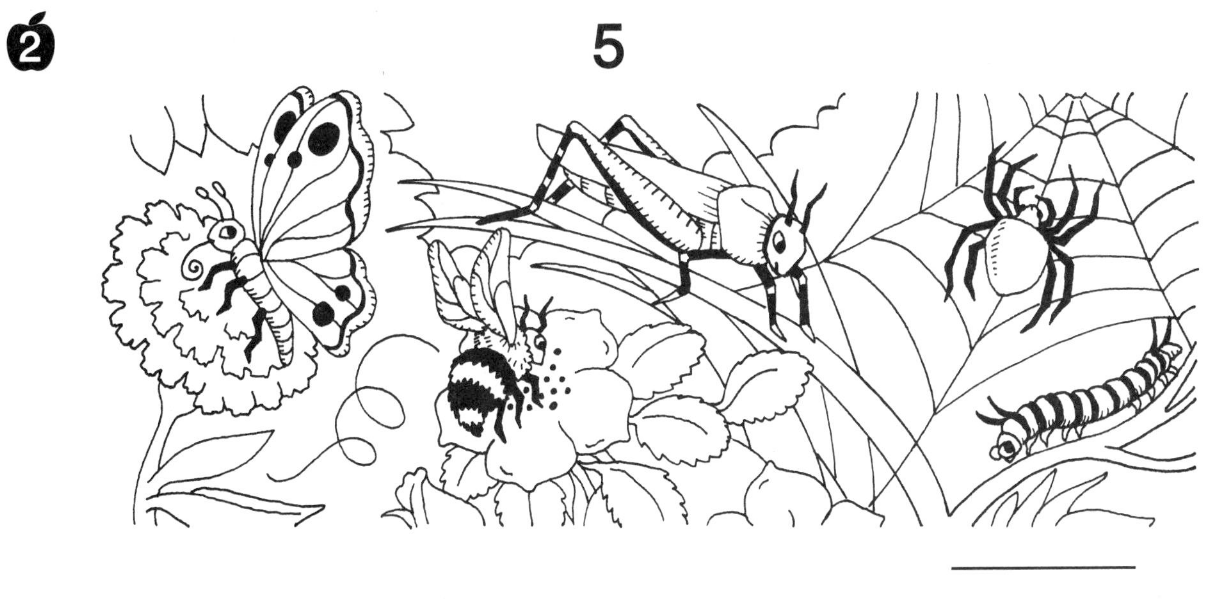

2 fewer than 5 is ________.

Directions In Exercise 1 have children count the number of baby and adult rabbits in each group and record the number. Have children compare the numbers and circle the number that is more. In Exercise 2 have children choose 2 favorite insects and mark an X on each. Then ask children to count how many insects are left and record the number.

Name ____________________

Stories About Joining

P 10-1

______ and ______ is ______.

Directions Have children color the small plants red, the large plants blue, and write the total number of each color in the number sentence. Then have children complete the sentence by writing the number of plants in all.

Name ____________________

Joining Groups

5 and 1 is 6.

2

____ and ____ is ____.

3

____ and ____ is ____.

Directions In each exercise have children write how many animals there are in each group. Then have them circle the 2 groups and record how many there are altogether.

Name ______________________

Draw a Picture

______ and ______ is ______.

______ and ______ is ______.

Directions Have children draw 2 more objects in each exercise. Ask children to write the numbers that tell how many there are in each group and how many there are altogether.

Name ______________________________

Using the Plus Sign

P 10-4

2 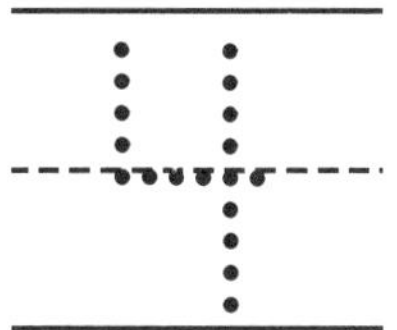 4

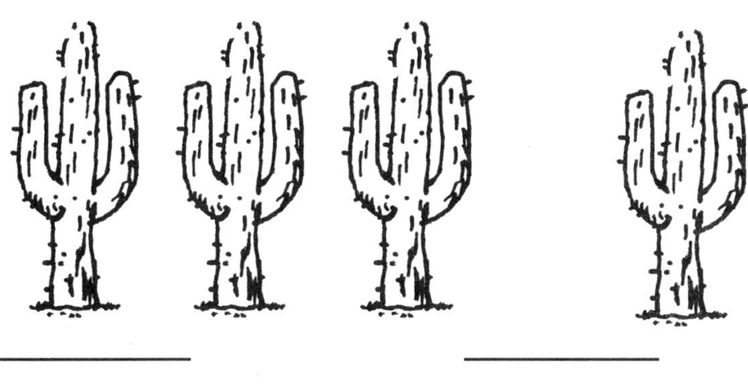

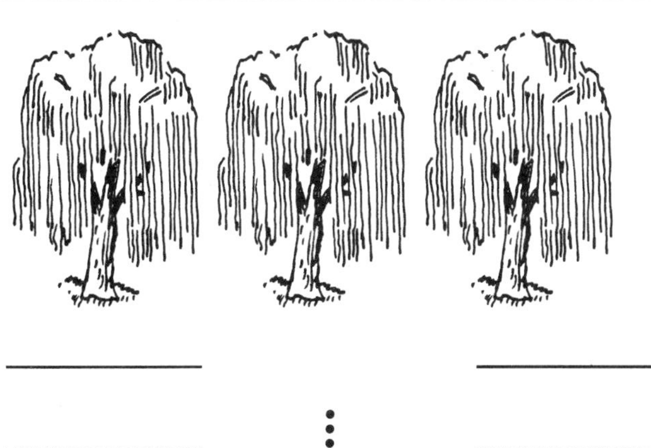

Directions In each exercise have children write how many there are in each group and circle the two groups to join them. Then have children write the plus sign and tell how many there are in all.

Name ______________________________

Finding the Sum

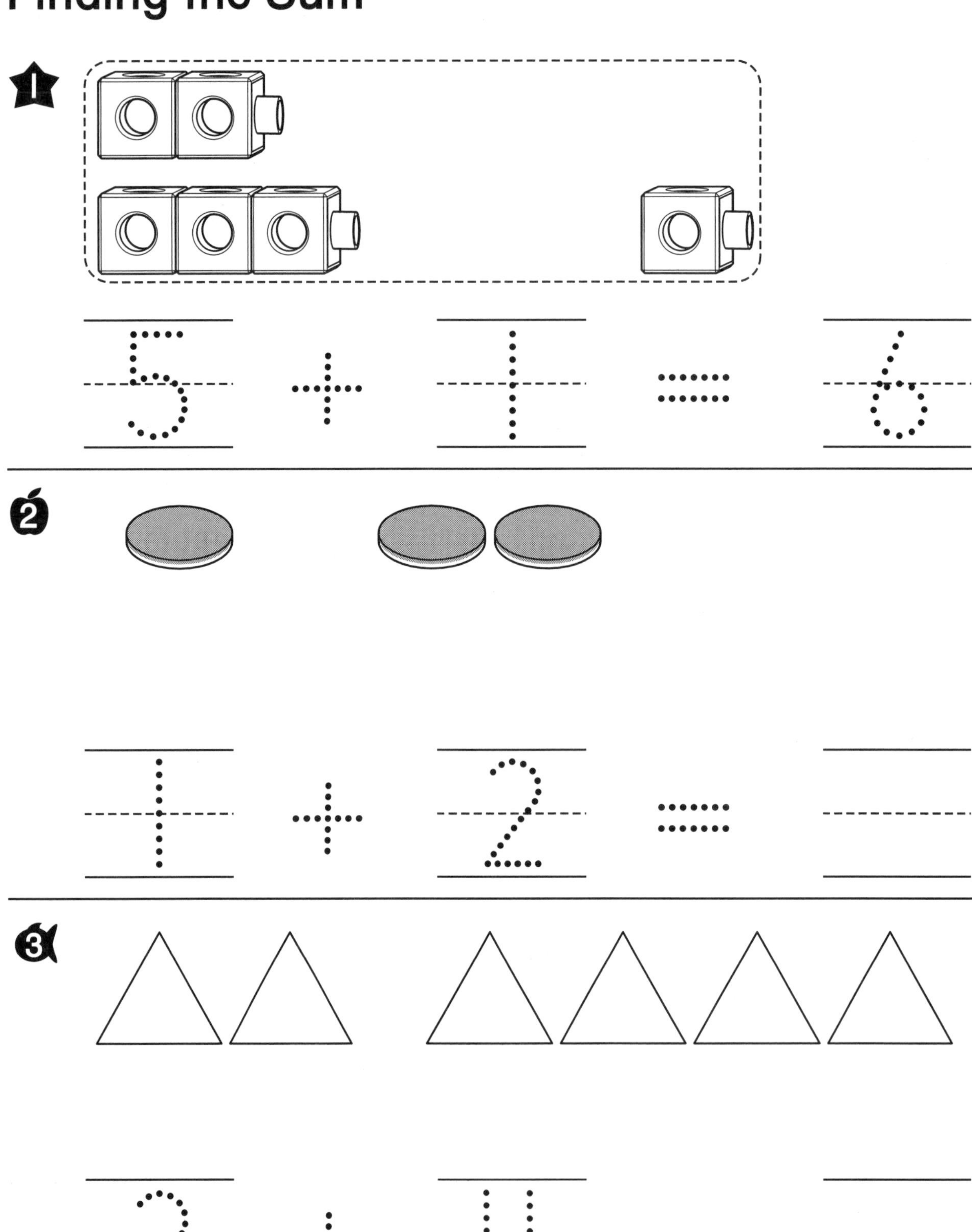

Directions In each exercise have children write how many there are in each group and circle the two groups to join them. Then have children write the plus and equal signs and record the sum.

Name ______________________________

Addition Sentences

P 10-6

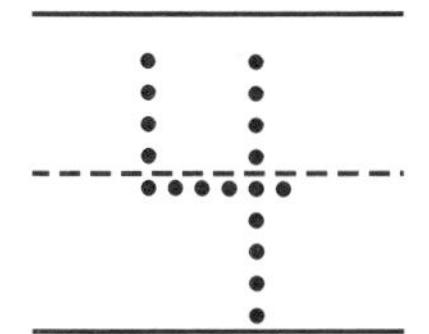 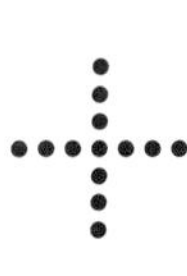 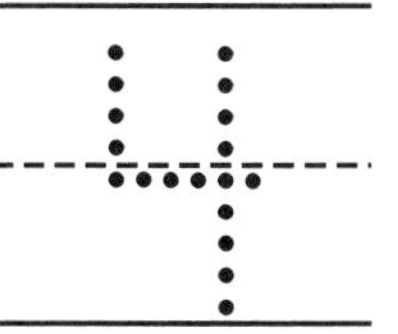  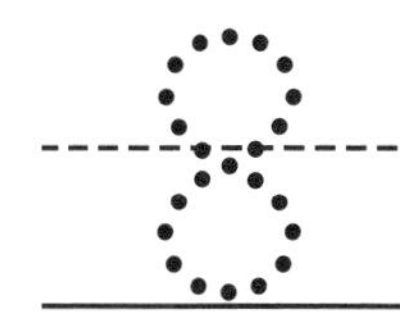

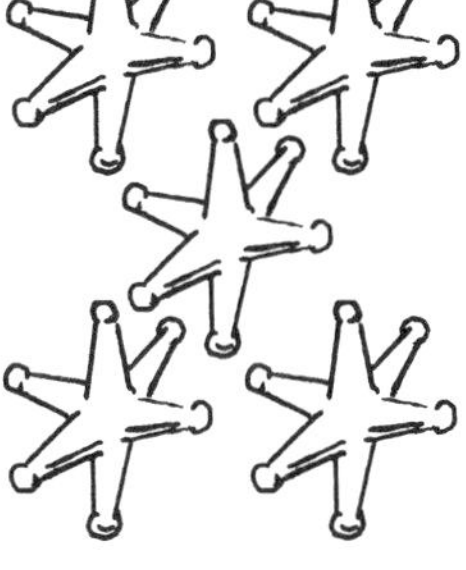

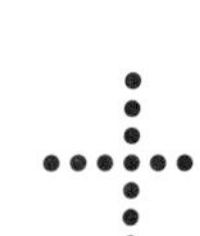

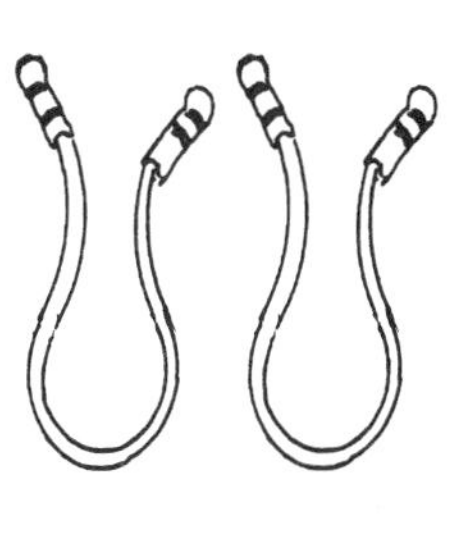

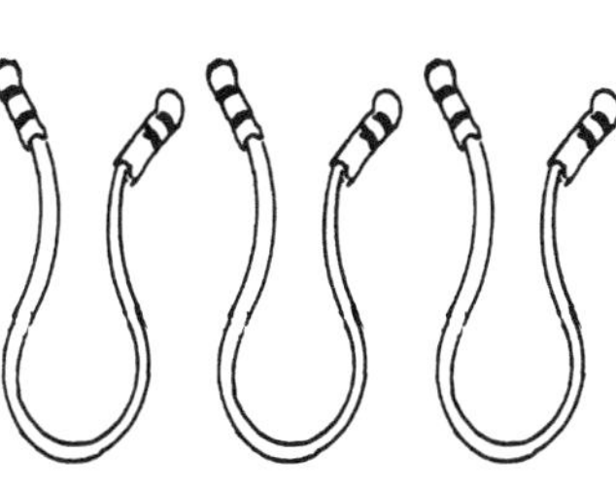

 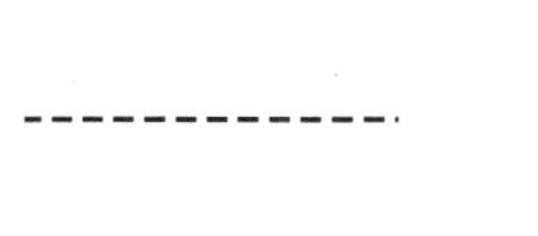

Directions In each exercise have children write how many there are in each group and circle the two groups to join them. Then have children complete the addition sentence by writing the plus and equal signs and recording the sum.

Name ____________________

Adding Pennies

P 10-7

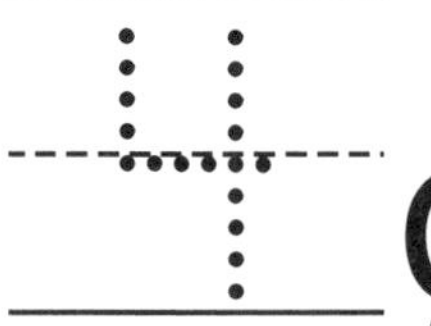

2 ¢ + 4 ¢ = 6 ¢

____ ¢ + ____ ¢ = ____ ¢

3

____ ¢ + ____ ¢ = ____ ¢

Directions In each exercise have children write how many pennies there are in each group, add the pennies, and complete the addition sentence by writing how many pennies there are in all.

Name ____________________

Look Alikes

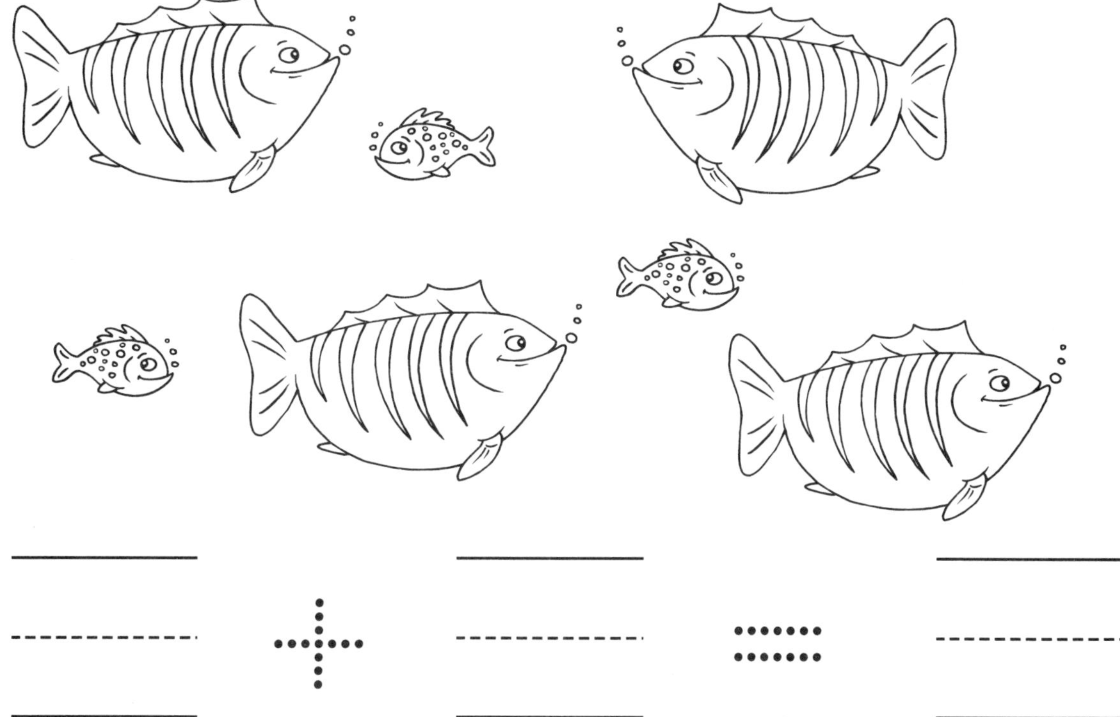

____ + ____ = ____

____ + ____ = ____

Directions In each exercise have children describe ways in which the animals are alike and different. Challenge them to figure out how to sort the animals in each exercise into 2 groups. Have children add the groups and write the addition sentence.

Name ____________________

Separating

____

________ are left.

____

________ are left.

Directions In each exercise have children place a counter on each animal in both groups and count how many there are in all. Have children remove counters for the group that is leaving, count how many are left, and record the number. Have partners tell each other stories about the pictures.

Name ______________________

Take Away

P 11-2

1. 7 take away 3 is 4.

2. ______ take away 3 is ______.

3. ______ take away 4 is ______.

4. ______ take away 2 is ______.

Directions Have children place matching tiles in Exercise 1 and write how many there are in all. Have them mark Xs as they take away 3 tiles. Then have children write how many are left. Repeat, having children take away 3 tiles in Exercise 2, 4 tiles in Exercise 3, and 2 tiles in Exercise 4.

Name ________________________________

Comparing

P 11-3

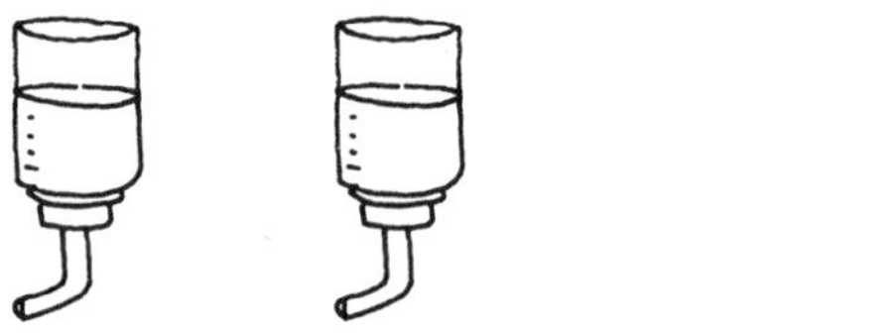

____

- - - - - - - - - - - -

________ fewer

2

____

- - - - - - - - - - - -

________ fewer

3

____

- - - - - - - - - - - -

________ fewer

Directions In each exercise have children draw a line to match each animal in one group to each item in the other group. Have them compare the groups, circle the group with fewer, and record how many fewer.

Name ______________________________

Using the Minus Sign

P 11-4

Directions In Exercise 1 have children write how many animals there are in all and mark an X to take away 1. Then have children write the minus sign, record the number taken away, and tell how many are left. Repeat, having children take away 2 in Exercise 2 and take away 3 in Exercise 3.

Name ____________________

Finding the Difference

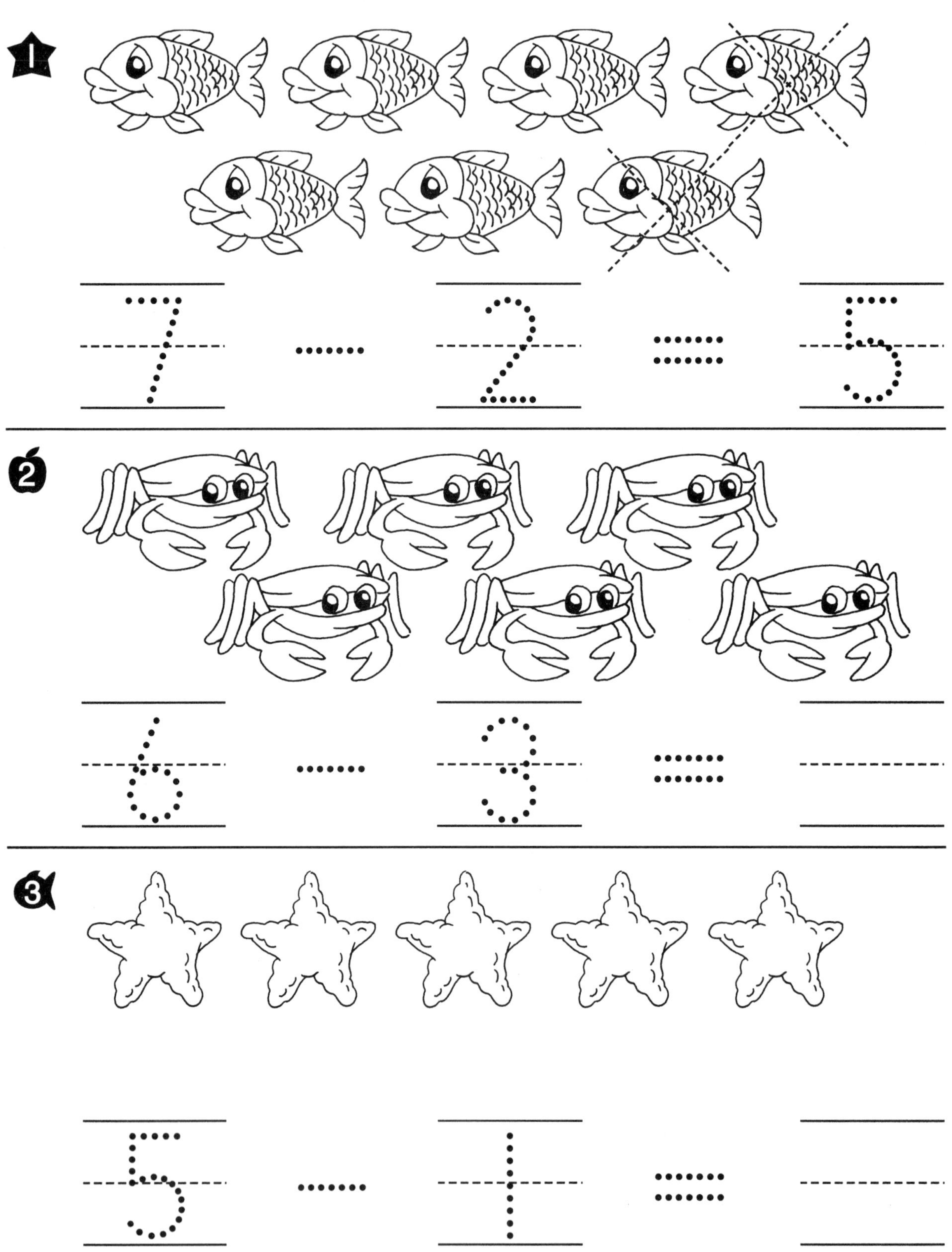

Directions In Exercise 1 have children write how many there are in all and mark Xs to take away 2. Have children write the minus sign and record the number taken away. Then have children write the equal sign and record the difference. Repeat, having children take away 3 in Exercise 2 and take away 1 in Exercise 3.

Name ______________________

Subtraction Sentences

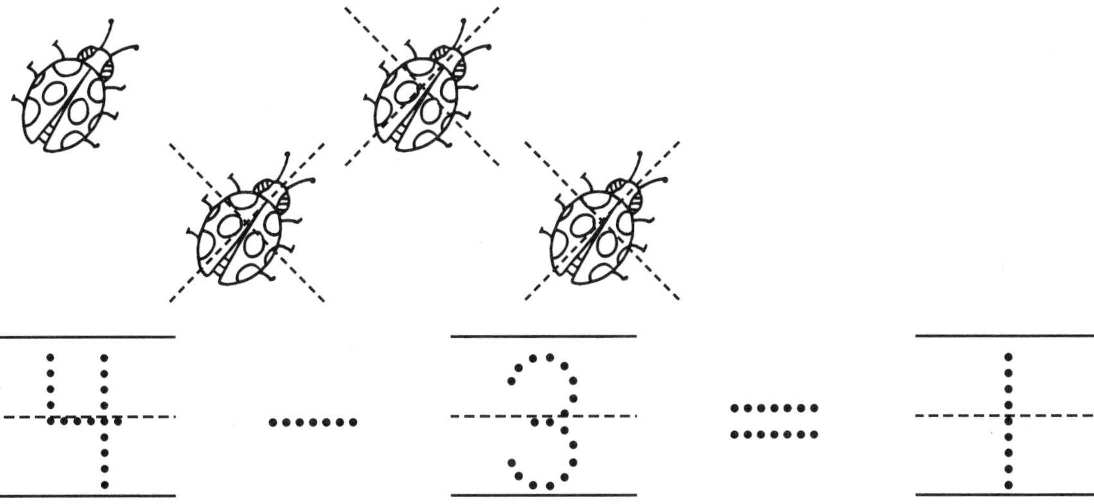

4 – 3 = 1

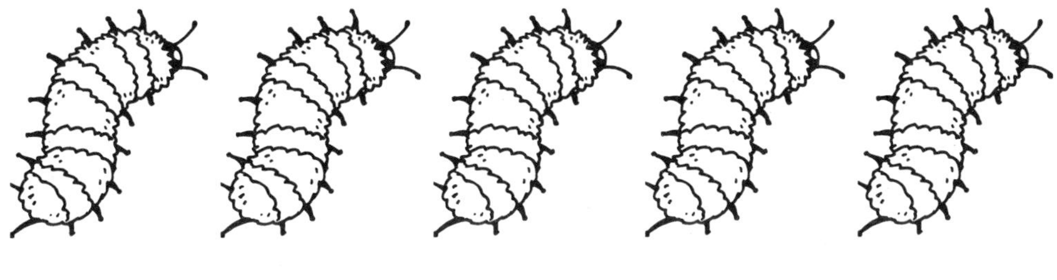

___ – ___ = ___

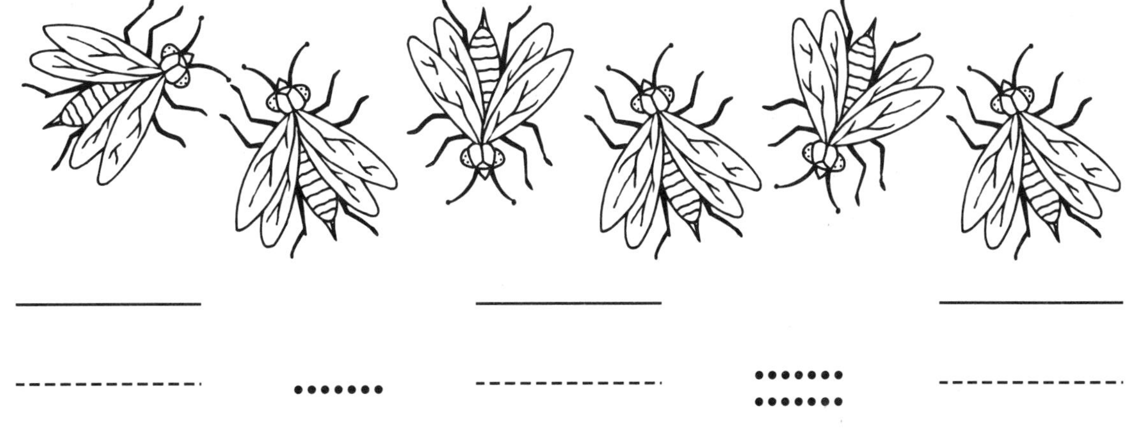

___ – ___ = ___

Directions In Exercise 1 have children write how many there are in all and mark Xs to take away 3. Have children write the minus sign and record the number taken away. Then have children complete the subtraction sentence by writing the equal sign and recording the difference. Repeat, having children take away 3 in Exercise 2 and take away 1 in Exercise 3.

Name ____________________

Subtracting Pennies

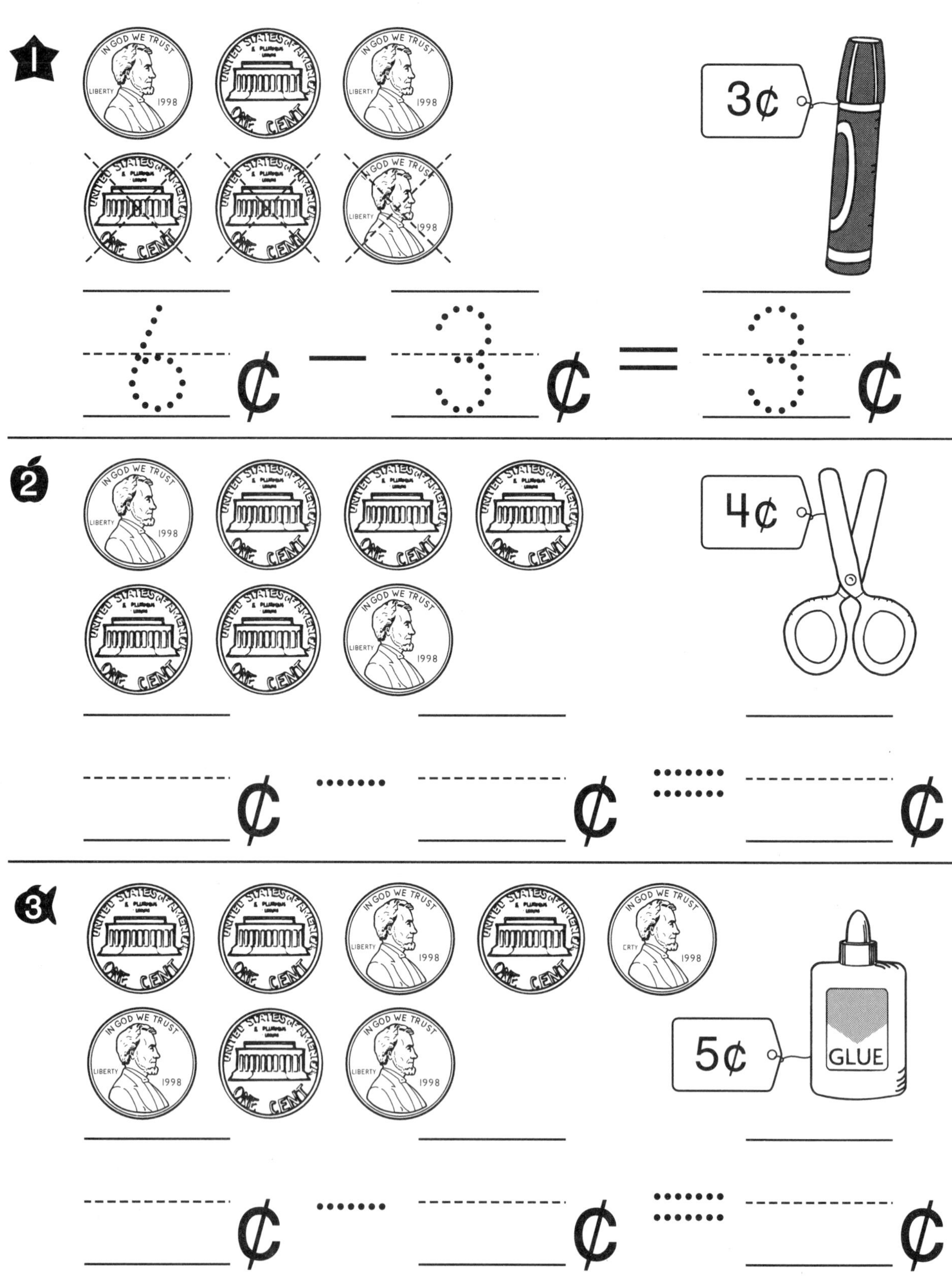

Directions In each exercise have children write how many pennies there are in all and mark Xs to show how many pennies they would use to buy the item. Then have children complete the subtraction sentence.

Name ______________________________

PROBLEM-SOLVING SKILL **P 11-8**

Choose an Operation

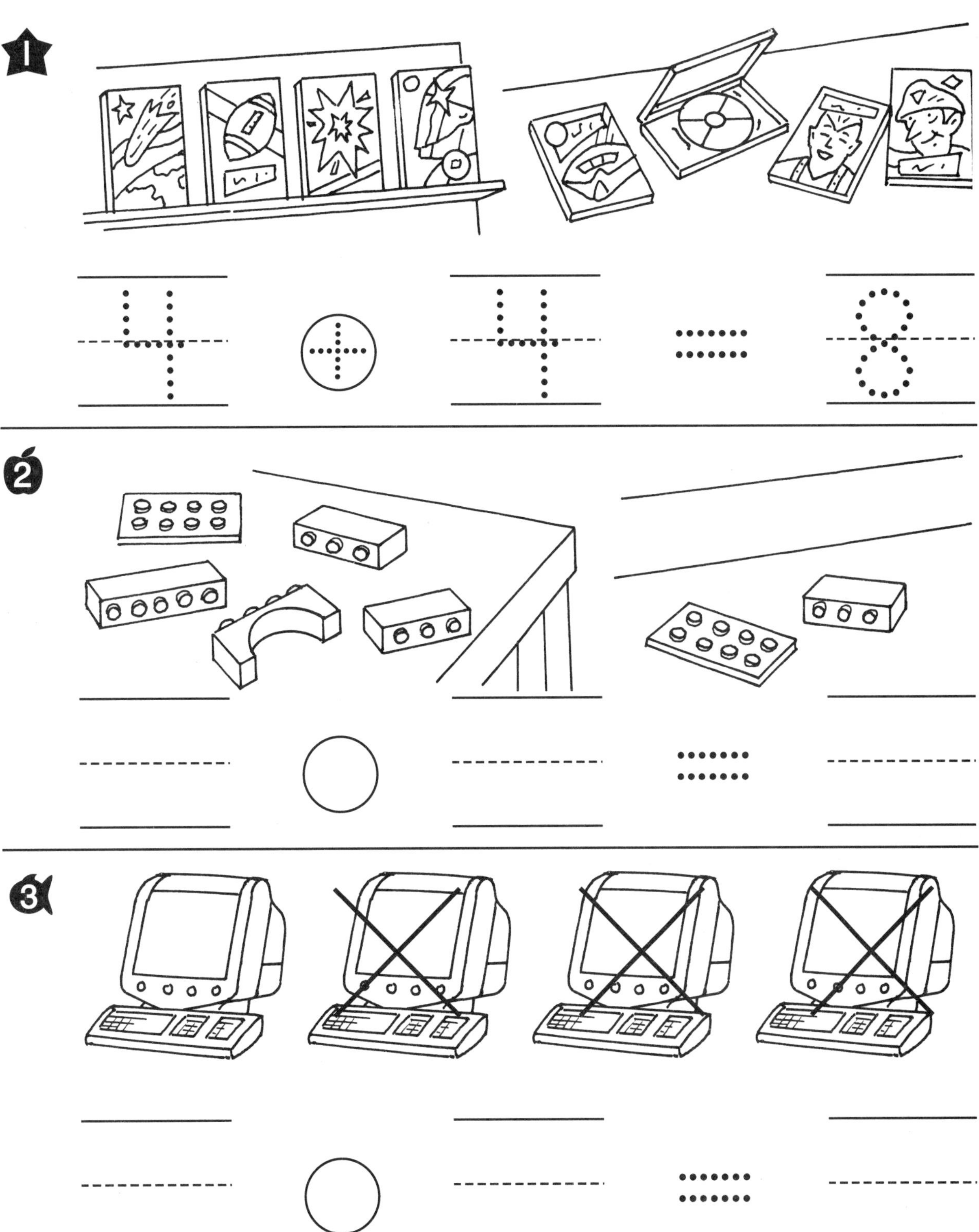

Directions In each exercise have children look at the pictures and decide whether to add or subtract. Then have children complete the addition or subtraction sentence.

Name ______________________________

PROBLEM-SOLVING APPLICATIONS **P 11-9**

Walk, Swim, or Fly

_______ ○ _______ ⊖ _______

Directions Talk with children about the pictures, pointing out that some of the animals fly while others swim. **How many of the animals fly?** Guide children to write the subtraction sentence that answers the question.

Name ________________________________

Counting Groups of 10

P 12-1

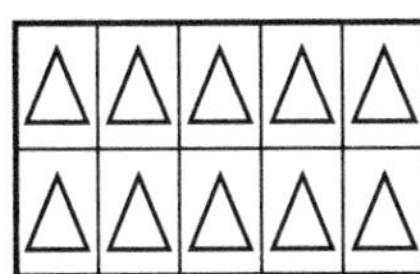
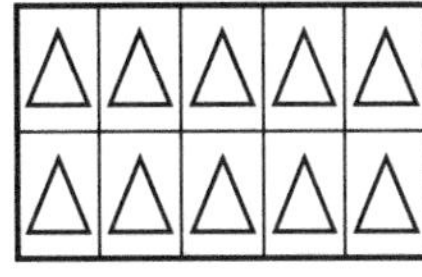
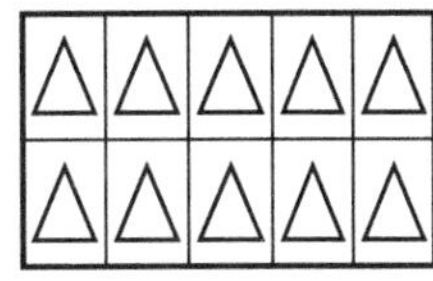
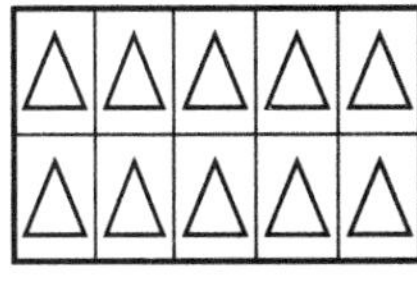

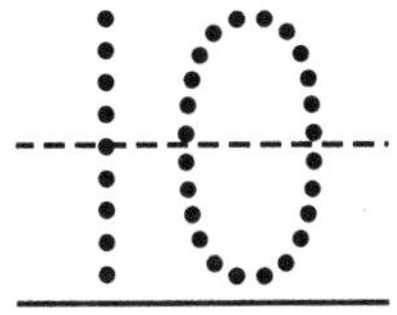
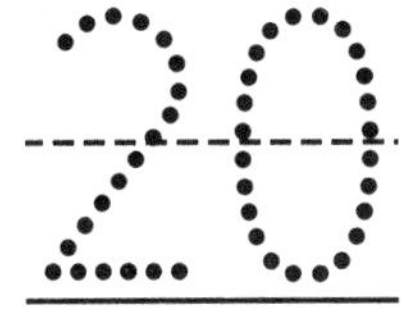

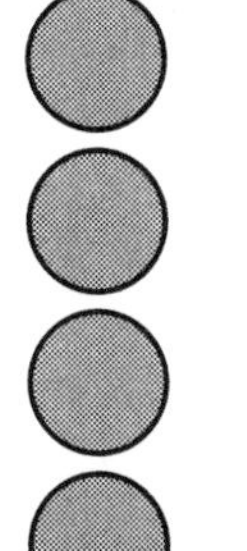
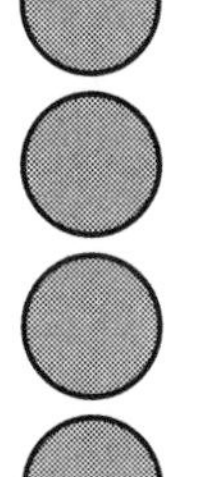
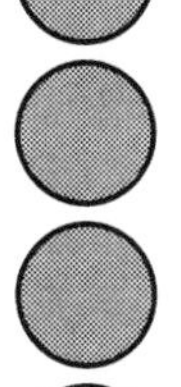
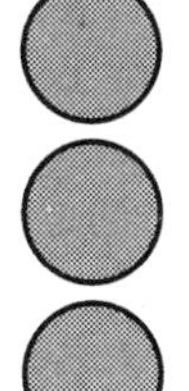
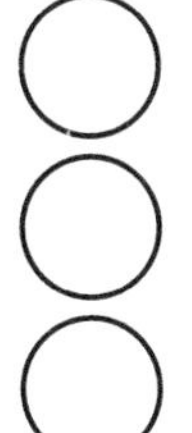

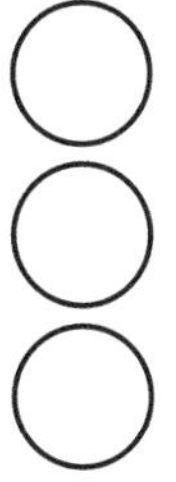

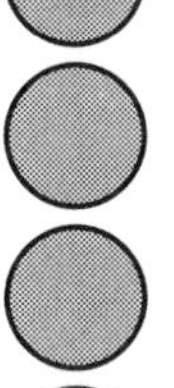
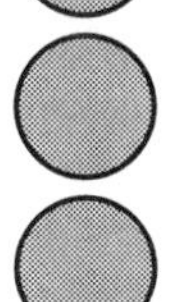

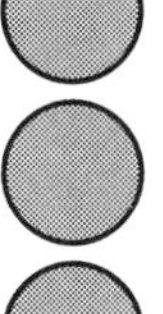
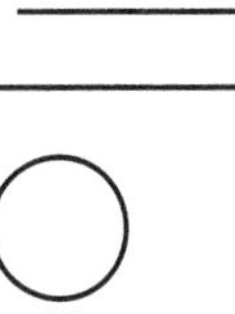

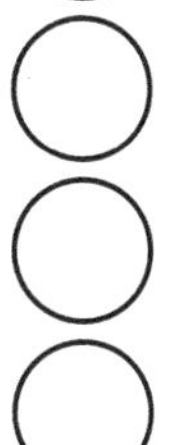
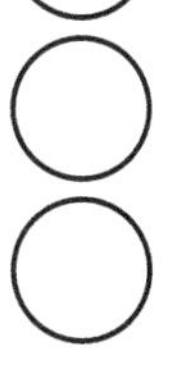

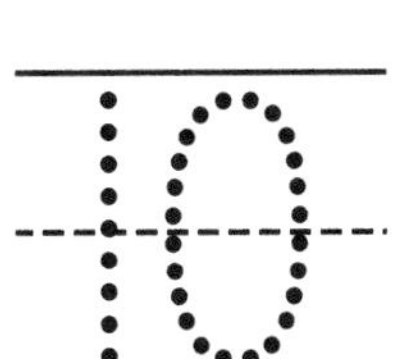
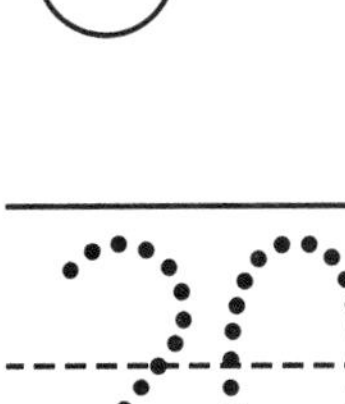

Directions In each exercise have children count the groups of 10 and write the numbers.

Name ______________________________

Numbers to 100

P 12-2

1	2	3	4	5	6	7	8	9	10
11	12	13	14	15	16	17	18	19	20
21	22	23		25	26		28	29	30
	32	33	34	35	36	37	38		40
41		43	44	45		47	48	49	50
51	52		54		56	57	58	59	60
61		63	64	65	66	67	68	69	
71	72			75	76	77	78	79	80
81	82	83	84			87	88	89	90
91		93	94	95	96	97		99	100

Directions Have children count to 100 on the hundred chart and write the missing numbers.

Name ______________________________

Counting Large Quantities

P 12-3

1

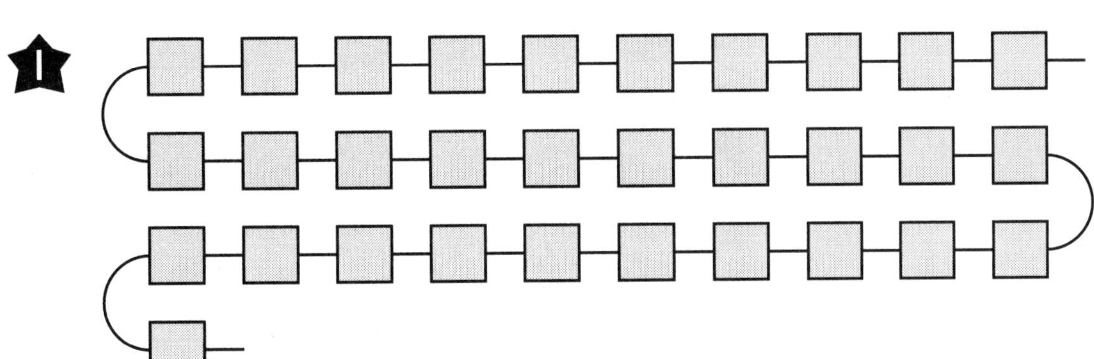

______

How many? ______

2

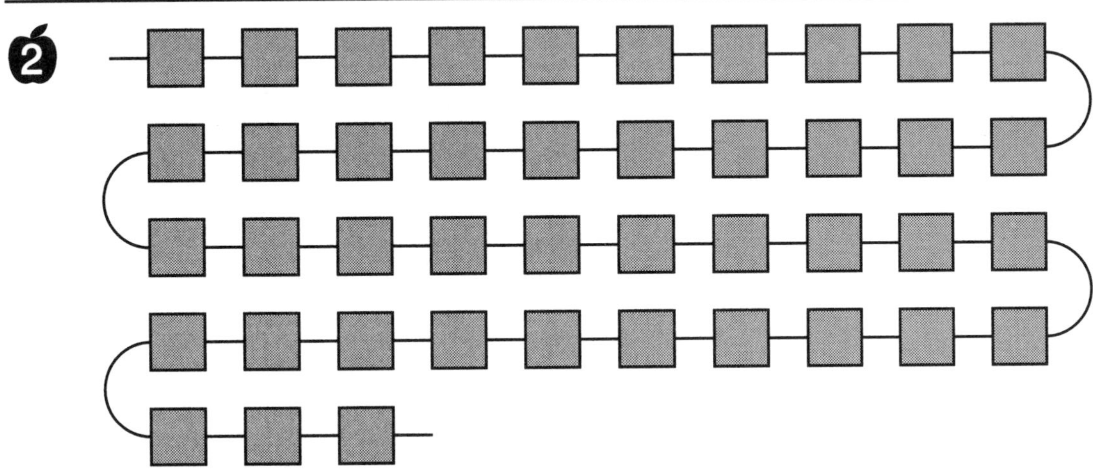

______

How many? ______

Directions In each exercise ask children to count the groups of 10 beads and then count on the remaining beads. Have children record how many beads there are.

Name ____________________

2s, 5s, and 10s on the Hundred Chart

P 12-4

1	2	3	4	5	6	7	8	9	10
11	12	13	14	15	16	17	18	19	20
21	22	23	24	25	26	27	28	29	
31	32	33	34	35	36	37	38	39	
41	42	43	44	45	46	47	48	49	
51	52	53	54	55	56	57	58	59	
61	62	63	64	65	66	67	68	69	
71	72	73	74	75	76	77	78	79	
81	82	83	84	85	86	87	88	89	
91	92	93	94	95	96	97	98	99	

Directions Have children count by 10s on the hundred chart and write the numbers. Then have children count by 5s and use a red crayon to color the numbers they counted.

Name ______________________________

Counting by 2s, 5s, and 10s

P 12-5

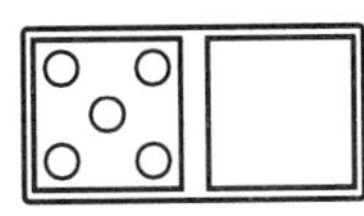 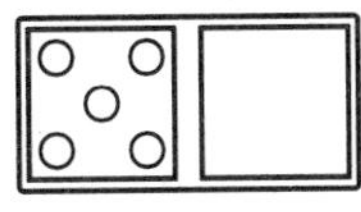 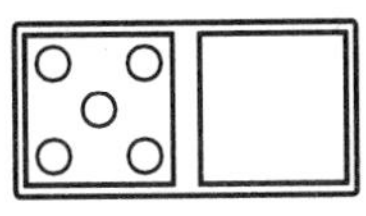 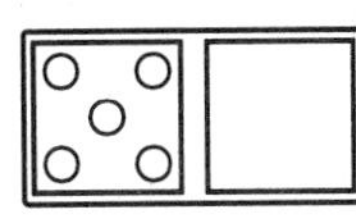 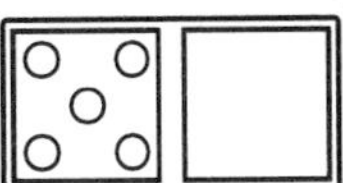

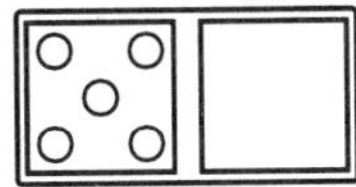 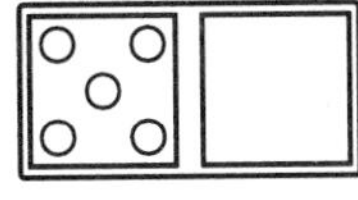 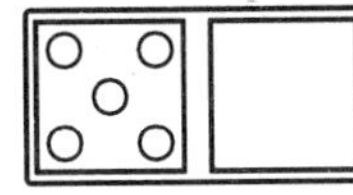 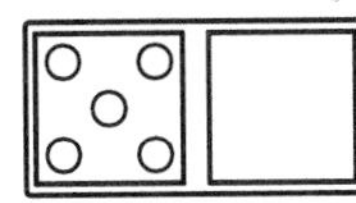

How many? ______

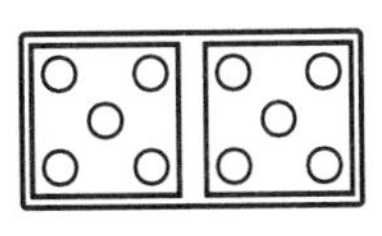 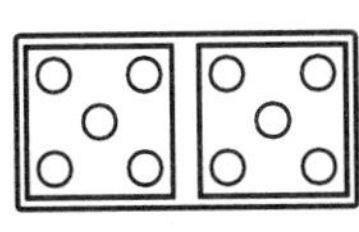 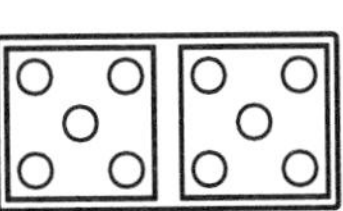 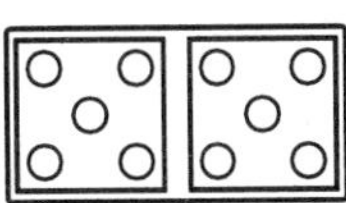 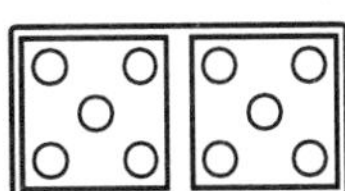

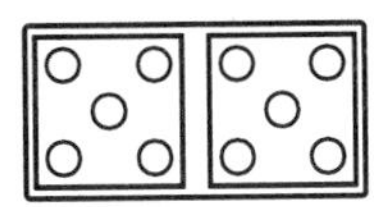 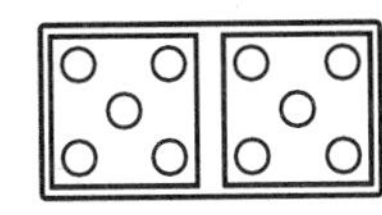

How many? ______

3

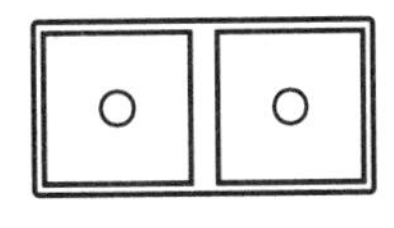 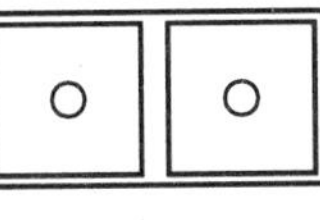 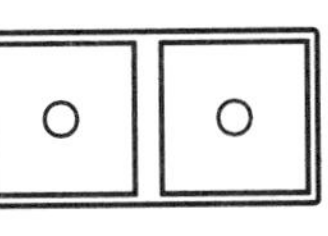 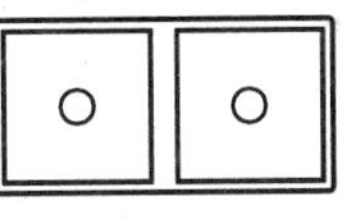 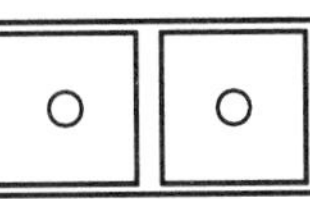

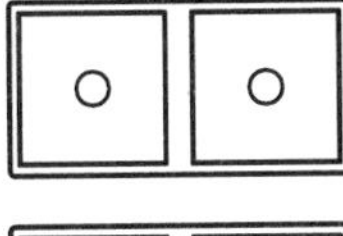 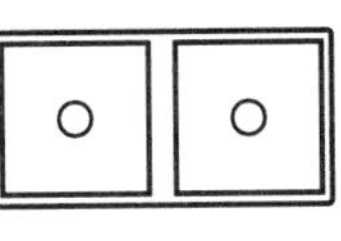 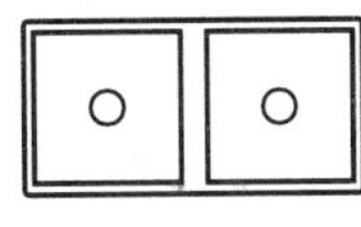 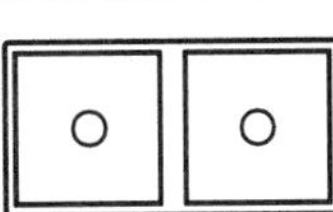

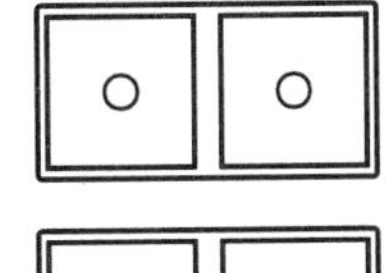 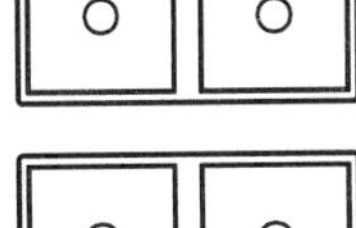 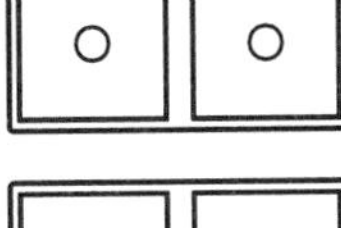 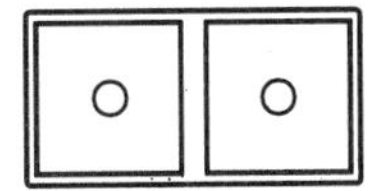

How many? ______

Directions In Exercise 1 have children count by 5s and record how many. In Exercise 2 have children count by 10s and record how many. In Exercise 3 have children count by 2s and record how many.

Name ______________________________

PROBLEM-SOLVING STRATEGY **P 12-6**

Look for a Pattern

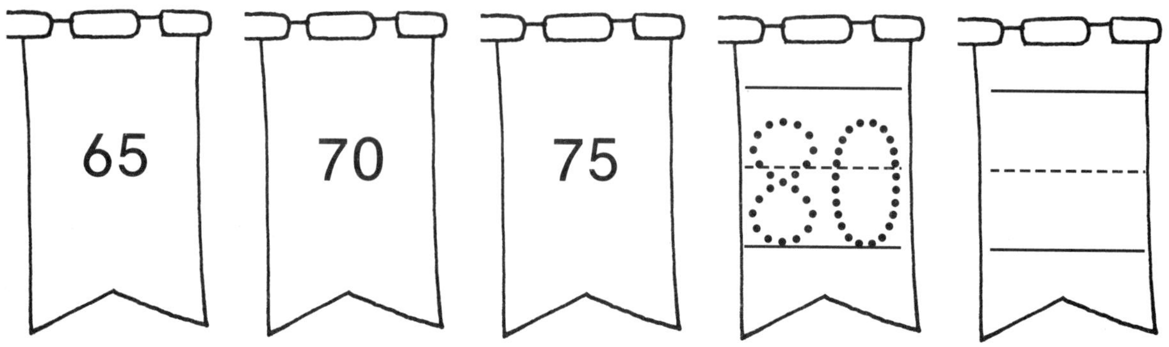

Directions In each exercise have children identify the number pattern and then continue the pattern by writing the missing numbers.

Name ______________________________

Nature Walk

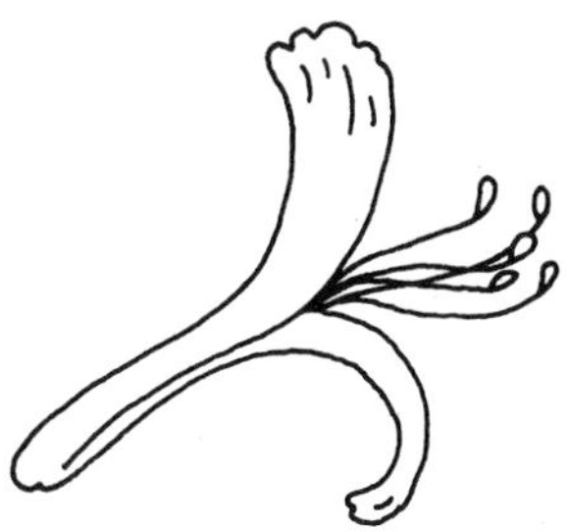

Honeysuckle

______ petals

Orchid

______ petals

Tulip

______ petals

Red Lily

______ petals

Columbine

______ petals

Directions Talk about the pictures, pointing out that flowers have unique petals. **How many petals do these flowers have?** Ask children to count the petals in each flower, write the numbers, and tell how they counted.